BEHIND THE SHIELD

The Police in Urban Society

BEHIND THE SHIELD

The Police in Urban Society

BY ARTHUR NIEDERHOFFER

Doubleday & Company, Inc.
Garden City, New York
1967

Acknowledgments

This work is the crystallization of more than twenty years of police experience ranging from pounding a beat to instructing recruits at the Police Academy. To supplement personal experience I interviewed police officers from many parts of the country. Since retirement I have maintained close contact with law enforcement, and for several years I taught police administration courses in the Law Enforcement and Correctional Administration program at New York University Graduate School of Public Administration.

The great majority of policemen are men of integrity and good will. Yet it is a fact that a minority "goes wrong." Why this should occur even to the extent that it does among a body of men so carefully selected, so well trained, and so strictly supervised, is a mystery, but one that will, I hope, be less an enigma by the time the reader comes to the last page of this book.

I cannot emphasize too strongly that this book should not be considered a critique aimed at the New York City Police Department. If I have frequently used the New York police as an illustration, this is no more than natural. It is a fine department, and I am proud to have worn its uniform. But it is my conviction that the points I make are generally true of large urban police forces in the United States today.

For New York City the reader may substitute Chicago, Philadelphia, Birmingham, Los Angeles, or Berkeley.

I want to express my appreciation to those who have been so generous with their help: Professors Leonard S. Cottrell, Jr., Robert Bierstedt, and Joseph Bram of New York University; Professor John McNamara of Santa Clara University; Professor Alfred Lee of Brooklyn College; and especially Doubleday Editor Anne Freedgood.

Finally, I must thank the members of my family. Martin contributed his magisterial wisdom. Birdie did a magnificent job of typing the many undecipherable handwritten pages. My wife Elaine was the perfect consultant, never failing to produce the proper thought or expression when it was needed. I dedicate this book to Elaine and to our children: Victor, Diane, and Roy.

Contents

BEHIND THE SHIELD

The Police in Urban Society

INTRODUCTION

From Station House to Glass House

The policeman is a "Rorschach" in uniform as he patrols his beat. His occupational accouterments—shield, nightstick, gun, and summons book—clothe him in a mantle of symbolism that stimulates fantasy and projection. Children identify with him in the perennial game of "cops and robbers." Teenagers in autos stiffen with compulsive rage or anxiety at the sight of the patrol car. To people in trouble the police officer is a savior. In another metamorphosis the patrolman becomes a fierce ogre that mothers conjure up to frighten their disobedient youngsters. At one moment the policeman is hero, the next, monster.

This dramatic impact has been camouflaged under a set of demeaning caricatures that stereotype members of the police force as sullen, stupid, or ridiculous. This "safety valve" helps the public to deprecate the wide authority of the individual policeman, and what is more important, causes it to overlook the ominous might of the police system. But this devaluation is no longer possible. Climactic social upheavals in America have thrust the police to the center of the public arena where their vital significance cannot be ignored.

The political fact is that police action was the immediate cause of the disastrous series of racial disturbances in Rochester, Philadelphia, Harlem, Hough, and Watts. Here, police confronted minority groups on opposite sides of the barricades. The intimate connection between law enforcement and the fate of our society was spelled out clearly as far back as Little Rock, Oxford, Birmingham, and Selma.

Nowhere was the might of the police establishment unsheathed more spectacularly than in the political struggle over the Civilian Review Board in New York City. By clever legal maneuvering the Patrolmen's Benevolent Association succeeded in submitting the question of a review board to the public. By a two-to-one majority in the November 1966 election the people of New York abolished the board that had been operating since the previous July. It was not clear whether the vote was in favor of the police or was a backlash against minority groups. But nevertheless, the magnitude of this victory can be measured only by the caliber of the opposition who fought to save the Review Board. They are the most powerful political leaders in the state—Senators Robert F. Kennedy and Jacob K. Javits, and Mayor John V. Lindsay.

In the legal sector the police are solidly aligned against the United States Supreme Court which, they suspect, is slowly but surely dismantling the hallowed foundation of law enforcement. The mores of our society teach us (and the police fiercely defend this view) that the principal function of the police system is prevention of crime and its deterrence. But it is apparent that a more idealistic philosophy of law enforcement is winning support in law schools and appellate courts. Professor Alexander M. Bickel of Yale Law School has summarized the new approach.

> But if it is remembered that the prime function of the criminal law is to encourage and sustain civilized conduct, to declare and confirm the basic moral code, then the justice and evenness of its administration, the decent and civilized calm and self-consistent manner in which it is brought

to bear are crucial to the attainment of its objectives, and are of a much higher order of importance than considerations of the speed and effectiveness with which we can process large numbers of cases to a successful "enforcement" conclusion.[1]

To the police the struggle over the Civilian Review Board and the recent trend of the Supreme Court decisions are proof of the breakdown of respect for law and order and their natural tendency is to close ranks against what appears to be a common enemy. But such solidarity is difficult to attain because within the police organization a revolution in theory and practice has left its mark in simmering internecine conflict. The vanguard of this radical change was a small but articulate elite composed for the most part of the younger superior officers who were college graduates. They acknowledged that allegations of inefficiency, corruption, and brutality were sometimes justified, and they set in operation a plan to put their house in order, a plan that can be described in one word—professionalism. Its blueprint was to establish high standards of selection, training, and performance, and to ensure that the force functioned at that level.

The new professionals were soon locked in a struggle for control against the conservative defenders of traditional police mores. Centripetal pressures prevented a complete rupture between the contending parties. The supporters of the old regime could not remain implacably hostile toward every proposal of their opponents, especially in those areas that might lead to higher salaries, greater prestige, and increased autonomy. The professionals were more liberal and tolerant, but they were policemen first, so they could not show themselves "soft" on minority-group action that verged on viola-

[1] Cited in Irving R. Kaufman, "The Confession Debate Continues," New York *Times Magazine*, October 2, 1966, p. 87.

tion of law. They also felt obliged to defend the police occupation against further constraints at the hands of the United
States Supreme Court. Nor could they permit any diminu-
tion of their professional autonomy, and for this reason they
were against the concept of a civilian-dominated review
board. On these issues the professionals stood shoulder to
shoulder with the factions opposing them within the police
organization. Therefore, ambivalence tempered the internal
war.

From within the system a conflict of values is spreading
confusion. The old police code symbolized by the "tough
cop" is waning. The new ideology glorifying the "social
scientist police officer" is meeting unexpected resistance. The
external force of social change has set the police organization
adrift in uncharted territory. When a bureaucracy founders,
the unfortunate victims are the men in the lower ranks.

Until recently sociology was also guilty of neglecting the
police institution as a topic for scientific research,[2] although
it offered a made-to-order case of institutional split personality with the additional interesting feature that the occupation
was in the throes of a crusade to raise its lower-class status
to that of a profession. Obviously, this involved problems of
bureaucracy, professionalization, ideology, role conflict, social control, and occupational *anomie*—all subjects dear to
the heart and art of the sociologist.

One reason, perhaps, for the apparent lack of interest on
the sociologists' part may have been the "blue curtain" of
secrecy that screened most police organizations and prevented
the researcher from gaining the necessary entrée into the life
and world of the police. Only today is there a glimmer of

---

[2] In the twenty-five year period from 1940 to 1965 only six articles re-
motely concerned with the police were published in the *American Journal
of Sociology* and the *American Sociological Review*, the two major sociological journals.

change to a "glass house" concept that may dispel the wall of secrecy that is both a moral imperative and a formal rule and regulation:

> Policemen are under explicit orders not to talk about police work with anyone outside the department; there is much in the nature of a secret society about the police; and past experience has indicated that to talk is to invite trouble from the press, the public, the administration, and their colleagues.[3]

Sociologist Daniel Glaser has called attention to another, more subtle motive for the well-established resistance of police forces to any suggestion of study by outsiders—the fear of learning too much about themselves. The police prefer to keep this truth "out of their conscious conceptions of themselves."[4]

In contrast to the sociologists, several leading psychologists have found policemen to be a fascinating subject of investigation. For example, Lewis Terman and Arthur Otis, who in 1916 tested thirty candidates for the police force of San Jose, California, concluded that twenty-one of the thirty were mentally inferior; only three had I.Q.s of 100 or better.[5]

Several years later, Louis Thurstone conducted a similar study of the Detroit police force. To his surprise, superior officers did not do as well as the patrolmen who served

[3] William A. Westley, "The Police: A Sociological Study of Law, Custom, and Morality" (unpublished doctoral dissertation, University of Chicago, 1951), p. 30. See also William A. Westley, "Secrecy and the Police," *Social Forces*, Vol. 34 (1956), pp. 254–257. Not secrecy, which implies active resistance to exposure, but seclusion of the police function in the administration of justice is the danger seen in Jerome H. Skolnick, *Justice Without Trial: Law Enforcement in Democratic Society* (New York: John Wiley and Sons, Inc., 1966), p. 14.

[4] Daniel Glaser, "The Sociological Approach to Crime and Correction," *Law and Contemporary Problems*, Vol. 23 (Autumn, 1958), pp. 683–702.

[5] Lewis Terman, *et al.*, "A Trial of Mental and Pedagogical Tests in a Civil Service Examination for Policemen and Firemen," *Journal of Applied Psychology*, Vol. 1 (1917), p. 21.

under them. His explanation for this paradoxical result was that the most intelligent men left the department for greener pastures and did not wait for promotion.[6]

Another unusual finding was obtained by Terman and Catherine Miles in a study of a California police force. Unexpectedly, they discovered that the policemen ranked low on the masculinity scale, so low that out of fifteen occupations, policemen scored just above editors, clergymen, and artists.[7] Thereupon, the two researchers sent questionnaires to prominent psychologists who had recently published in this field. Unanimously and monotonously the responses came back ranking policemen at the very top of the masculinity scale. Since Terman and Miles drew their conclusions from the protocols of twenty-two police respondents (thirteen originally and then nine more in replication), the inadequacy of the sample leaves the policeman's reputation for virility unscathed. If it proves anything at all, it is that even the "experts" share the commonly held stereotype of the policeman's unquestioned masculinity.

Planning a handbook of diagnostic projective tests, David Rapaport chose for his control group the most normal population he could imagine—members of the Kansas Highway Patrol Force, who were used as a base to measure and compare the deviant groups. The test results were at marked variance with the original assumption that the police group was an average normal one. Rapaport was forced to admit that the police group "if compared with a city population would have to be considered in some degree schizoid."[8]

[6] Louis L. Thurstone, "The Intelligence of Policemen," *Journal of Personnel Research*, Vol. 1 (1922), pp. 64–74.

[7] Lewis M. Terman and Catherine C. Miles, *Sex and Personality: Studies in Masculinity and Femininity* (New York: McGraw-Hill Book Co., 1936), pp. 164, 174–176, 456.

[8] David Rapaport, *Diagnostic Psychological Testing* (Chicago: The Yearbook Publishers, Inc., 1949), Vol. 1, p. 29.

A few years later Solis L. Kates administered Rorschach tests to twenty-five New York City patrolmen and found that the tests indicated that the more maladjusted policemen "tended to be more satisfied with their work than the less maladjusted."[9]

Sociologists must yield; they have rarely matched the eye-catching appeal of the psychological studies. The closest approach is a report on the police of twenty-five years ago by sociologist Read Bain in which he stated that three-quarters of the policemen in the United States were mentally unfit for their work.[10] In the classic analysis of race relations in the United States, Gunnar Myrdal's *American Dilemma*, there is this commentary on the Southern policeman: "Almost anyone on the outside of the penitentiary who weighs enough and is not blind or crippled can be considered as a police candidate."[11]

In England there is a more favorable image of the policeman. The British anthropologist Geoffrey Gorer has formulated some provocative hypotheses in which he suggests that the law-abiding English citizen has incorporated the policeman as a model and ideal for the superego.

> I wish to advance the hypothesis that one of the techniques by which the national character of a society may be modified or transformed over a given period is through the selection of personnel for institutions which are in continuing contact with the mass of the population in a somewhat superordinate position.[12]

[9] Solis L. Kates, "Rorschach Responses, Strong Blank Scales and Job Satisfaction among Policemen," *Journal of Applied Psychology*, Vol. 34 (1950), p. 252.

[10] Read Bain "The Policeman on the Beat," *The Scientific Monthly*, Vol. 48 (1939), p. 452.

[11] Gunnar Myrdal, *An American Dilemma* (New York: Harper and Brothers, 1944), pp. 538–539.

[12] Geoffrey Gorer, *Exploring English Character* (London: The Cresset Press, 1955), p. 305.

I should like to suggest that, increasingly during the past century, the English policeman has been for his peers not only an object of respect but also a model of the ideal male character, self controlled, possessing more strength than he ever has to call into use except in the gravest emergency, fair and impartial, serving the abstractions of Peace and Justice rather than any personal allegiance or sectional advantage.[13]

So that the bulk of the population has, so to speak, incorporated the police man or woman as an ideal and become progressively more "self policing."[14]

If the metaphor be allowed, the American has an incorporated school teacher as part of his or her superego, the English man or woman an incorporated policeman.[15]

If Gorer's contention has any merit, it provides one more compelling reason for a serious study of the policeman and the force of which he is the basic unit.

Unfortunately, in contrast to their English counterparts, the police in America have never been acclaimed as models for middle-class scions,[16] and they are acutely aware of this. The police feel that they deserve respect from the public. But the upper class looks down on them; the middle class seems to ignore them, as if they were part of the urban scenery; the lower class fears them. Even the courts often appear to be against them, making it more and more difficult to obtain convictions of criminals. With bitterness,

[13] Ibid., pp. 310–311.
[14] Geoffrey Gorer, "Modification of National Character: The Role of the Police in England," in Personal Character and Cultural Milieu, ed. Douglas G. Haring, (Syracuse: Syracuse University Press, 1956), p. 337.
[15] Ibid., p. 338.
[16] See Erik H. Erikson, Childhood and Society (New York: Norton, 1963), pp. 106–107 for a discussion of the popularity of the police role among 10- and 11-year-old boys in California. For an earlier reference to the policeman as part of the superego, not as a model but as a punitive figure, see Clyde Kluckhohn and Henry A. Murray, Personality in Nature, Society, and Culture (New York: Alfred A. Knopf, 1954), p. 44.

therefore, the police tend to think of themselves as a minority group in the society.[17]

When a group feels that it is being threatened, or treated unfairly, it falls back on its code of values. Cynicism is an ideological plank deeply entrenched in the ethos of the police world, and it serves equally well for attack or defense. For many reasons the police are particularly vulnerable to cynicism. When they succumb, they lose faith in people, society, and eventually in themselves. In their Hobbesian view the world becomes a jungle in which crime, corruption, and brutality are normal features of the terrain.

Such a philosophy, softened by a touch of compassion or a sense of humor, converts men into tolerant observers of the human comedy. Without these saving graces it leads to misanthropy, pessimism, and resentment—a dangerous combination, particularly in the case of policemen whose role clothes them with both power and ample opportunity to "act out" these underlying and largely unconscious orientations.[18]

There are at least four potential sources of cynicism in the police system. The young policeman may learn it as part of the socialization process, or absorb it through contact with an established police subculture. Or it may be that cynicism is a product of occupational *anomie*—a concept about which we shall have more to say. Finally, there may be something about the personalities of policemen that prepares the ground.

Cynicism is at the very core of police problems, and therefore the focus of the research study that is reported in the

[17] Skolnick found "that the policeman typically perceives the citizenry to be hostile to him." Jerome H. Skolnick, *op. cit.*, p. 62.

[18] The political scientist Harold D. Lasswell reaches a similar hypothesis in relation to the power seeker. He proposes that power becomes compensation for deprivation by overcoming low estimates of the self. Power accomplishes this result "by changing either the traits of the self or the environment in which it functions." See Harold D. Lasswell, *Power and Personality* (New York: The Viking Press, 1963), p. 39.

Appendix. Although the need for improvement in law enforcement is self-evident, it will not come about fortuitously. First we must comprehend the present reality of the police system. It is my hope that this book will encourage that vital confrontation.

CHAPTER I

The Urban Police Department: From Bureaucracy to Profession

Large urban police departments are bureaucracies. Members of the force sometimes lose their bearings in the labyrinth of hierarchy, specialization, competitive examinations, red tape, promotion based on seniority, impersonality, rationality, rules and regulations, channels of communication, massive files, and authority in one's office rather than in his person.[1]

Officially the function of the police organization is:

1. Protection of life and property.
2. Preservation of the peace.
3. Prevention of crime.
4. Detection and arrest of violators of law.
5. Enforcement of laws and ordinances.
6. Safeguarding the rights of individuals.[2]

But these primary duties are sometimes forgotten under the pressure of accomplishing the various licensing, inspecting,

[1] These criteria of bureaucracy have been gathered from the following sources: H. H. Gerth and C. Wright Mills, eds. *From Max Weber: Essays in Sociology* (New York: Oxford University Press, 1958), pp. 196–244; Robert K. Merton, *Social Theory and Social Structure* (Glencoe: The Free Press, 1957), pp. 195–224; Joseph Bensman and Bernard Rosenberg, *Mass, Class, and Bureaucracy* (Englewood Cliffs: Prentice-Hall, Inc., 1963), pp. 255–321; and Peter M. Blau, *Bureaucracy in Modern Society* (New York: Random House, 1956).

[2] J. Edgar Hoover, *Should You Go Into Law Enforcement?* (New York: New York Life Insurance Co., 1961), p. 7.

and administrative tasks required of the modern department. In addition, the police regulate traffic, combat vice and gambling, and try to cope with juvenile delinquency.

When we examine the function of the police in society, some thought-provoking conclusions emerge. Law enforcement policy is established by higher authority in the government and usually represents the interests of the power centers in the community. As Dan Dodson, the Director of the Center for Human Relations and Community Studies at New York University, put it:

> No policeman enforces all the laws of a community. If he did, we would all be in jail before the end of the first day. The laws which are selected for enforcement are those which the power structure of the community wants enforced. The police official's job is dependent upon his having radar-like equipment to sense what is the power structure and what it wants enforced as law.[3]

Joseph Lohman, Dean of the School of Criminology of the University of California at Berkeley, who was once a police officer himself, has gone even farther, declaring that

> The police function [is] to support and enforce the interests of the dominant political, social, and economic interests of the town, and only incidentally to enforce the law.[4]

These two observations recall the Communist dogma that the police of capitalist nations are "lackeys of the ruling class." They also underline the legitimate point that police systems can be understood only as institutions in interaction with the rest of the social structure. The power structure

[3] Dan Dodson, Speech delivered at Michigan State University, May 1955, reported in *Proceedings of the Institute on Police-Community Relations*, May 15–20, 1955 (East Lansing: The School of Police Administration and Public Safety, Michigan State University, 1956), p. 75.

[4] Westley, "The Police: A Sociological Study of Law, Custom, and Morality," *op. cit.*, p. 38.

and the ideology of the community, which are supported by the police, at the same time direct and set boundaries to the sphere of police action.

A rule of thumb which gives a proper perspective on the police system is one that I have named "the principle of equilibrium." It refers to an organizational imperative that requires the negation of any and all criticism. The two most popular methods of accomplishing this are to pile up a mass of exculpatory statistics in the next report; or to attack the reputation or motives of the critic and thus by an *argumentum ad hominem* to nullify both the critic and the criticism. Law enforcement has developed standards to measure its efficiency, but these are not sufficient. The record of performance must be validated by the stamp of public approval.

Thus a weather eye is always turned to the press and other mass media that police administrators perceive as dependable barometers of public opinion. If a newspaper column is favorable, all is rosy. If the report is critical, the response is predictable. Sometimes the results are fantastic. Occasionally, a well-known gossip columnist reports that "a floating crap game is now operating in the city," or a bookie, or a brothel. Immediately, the entire police bureaucracy is shocked into action by the implication of "neglect of duty." Orders emanate from the office of the Commissioner. Division and precinct commanders frantically instruct members of their commands to search every nook and cranny and then deliver a written report that the evildoers mentioned by the columnist are nowhere within the confines of the precinct. How many man-hours and how much money are expended in such pursuits will never be known.

Another example of the principle of equilibrium is the reliance on statistics. Every major police department spends a good portion of its time grinding out statistical reports:

statistics of arrests, summonses, warnings, convictions, ambulance calls, fatalities. Each case is transformed into a number and reported wherever possible in a manner that enhances the glory of the department. The contemporary trend to seek a cure for every personal problem in "analysis" has invaded the police bureaucracy. But whereas a patient in psychoanalysis supplies data by a stream of consciousness, it is the never-ending stream of statistics that symbolizes police case histories. The analysis unit is the main arm of defense in the struggle of the department to justify itself. In any emergency the chief frequently turns for help to this specialized police bureau.

Here, every day, crime is subjected to scholarly postmortem. Rape becomes a mathematical problem, murder a pale study in costs and larceny just a question of logistics. Drained of blood and fright, the figures progress through slide rule, tabulating equipment and typewriter and come out at the end in the department's annual eighty-page Statistical Digest.[5]

This was written as an encomium to the Los Angeles Police Department by one of its greatest admirers, Jack Webb, of Dragnet fame. Since his TV slogan was, "Give me the facts," it is probably no accident that he glorifies the statistical unit.

With monotonous regularity the statistics reported are collated, and often manipulated, so that they prove how successfully the department is performing its duties. If newspapers complain that delinquency is rising, the next police report will inevitably reveal a great increase in arrests of juvenile delinquents. When a safety council alleges that motorists are speeding dangerously, "by coincidence" the

[5] Jack Webb, *The Badge: The Inside Story of One of America's Great Police Departments* (Englewood Cliffs: Prentice-Hall, Inc., 1958), p. 84.

police publish statistics of a tremendous number of summonses issued for speeding violations.

Critics of the police have lost faith in police crime statistics.

> Crime statistics have always been an inside joke, a near-absurdity to criminologists, sociologists and like *cognoscenti*. Across the years law enforcement officials have orchestrated the figures and then played them as a fabulous concerto in numbers that served varying purposes depending on the occasion.[6]

Members of the force themselves realize that statistics are artificially regulated to make monthly and annual reports appear more impressive. When a commanding officer tells them that a new policy of enforcement is to be followed, the patrol force is skeptical, interpreting the purpose behind the change as the desire to build up a record on paper, rather than to meet the actual need for police services.

John Griffin, at the time a member of the Joint Committee on Curriculum and Personnel of the Police Science Program conducted by the New York City Police Department and the Baruch School of the City College of New York, confirmed this opinion. In a paper presented to the American Statistical Association at Stanford University in August 1960, Griffin is reported to have said:

> [The fact that] even police are cynical about the validity of crime statistics . . . reflects a long standing conviction in many police agencies that the truth should not be reported.
> There is inevitable pressure to close the squeal book. Police commanders know the best way to make crime control look better is to reduce the number of crimes reported.[7]

[6] Sidney Zion, "The Police Play a Crime Numbers Game," New York *Times*, June 12, 1966, Section IV, p. 6.

[7] San Francisco *News-Call Bulletin*, August 24, 1960. A former FBI agent has charged that the FBI's statistical image is "manufactured" in much the same way. See William W. Turner, "Crime Is Too Big for the FBI," *The Nation*, Vol. 201, November 8, 1965, p. 325.

Toward Professionalization

Until the Depression, membership in the police force was a monopoly of the lower class. In the 1930's, however, top-grade patrolmen in New York City earned three thousand dollars a year. They owned houses and automobiles; they could afford the luxuries that were the envy of the middle class; and they were never laid off. In the panic of the Depression the middle class began to regard a police career pragmatically. Young men chose police work in preference to occupations higher in the social scale because of the salary and the security. It was lucrative and less expensive to attain than the position of lawyer or teacher.

Municipal governments cooperated. They were delighted to obtain the better educated middle-class candidate. Entrance examinations were slanted in favor of college men. Instead of technical information, the tests stressed general knowledge and intelligence. Extra credit was given for college attendance and even for participation in college athletics. This was unquestionably unfair and discriminatory, but it accomplished its purpose. Police lists began to bulge with college graduates—teachers, engineers, lawyers, and even some near dentists and doctors. Of the three hundred recruits appointed to the New York City Police Department in June 1940, more than half held college degrees.[8] Police rookies of that class still remember the envy they incurred in apprentice lawyers earning five dollars a week and out-of-

[8] *Spring 3100*, Vol. 11 (October 1940), pp. 8, 9, 12, 13. As prosperity returned, the number of college graduates interested in becoming policemen fell off sharply. During the last decade men with college degrees have rarely reached 5 per cent of the average recruit class.

work teachers afraid to leave the telephone in case the rare call for a day of substitute teaching might come.

These middle-class college men formed the nucleus of the future elite group; before long they began to try to raise the prestige of the police occupation to match their own middle-class ideologies and attainments; to transform it into a profession.

The complexity of contemporary urban society coupled with technological advances provided another push toward professionalism. The modern police specialist requires a wide range of technical and scientific skills. Experts are needed to operate radar, photographic equipment, electronic listening devices, instruments for analysis of evidence, computers, complex office machines, radio, television, airplanes, and helicopters. The scientific devices used in detective investigations have created a corps of specialists, quasi-scientist technicians who consider themselves different from, and a little better than, beat patrolmen, and have thrown their support to professionalism.

Professionalism also appeals to the "thinking" policeman. The repeated investigations, which never fail to unearth graft and corruption, are a threat to the stability of the system. To the ancient query, *"Quis custodiet ipsos custodes?"* the best answer is professionalism because it can eventually win for the police the privilege of "self-policing."

For all these reasons the police occupation has for some time seemed ripe for professionalization. But within the ranks many of the less educated, tradition-directed members of the force continue to fight to preserve their hegemony. Dissension has reached serious proportions, verging on internecine class conflict between the lower-class conservatives and the upwardly mobile middle-class radicals.

The latter's goal is to give law enforcement a status nearly equal to that of the three classical professions, Law, Medicine, and Theology, on the ground that policemen share with lawyers, doctors, and clergymen a special privilege:

> all of them must have license to get—and, in some degree, to keep secret—some order of guilty knowledge. It may be guilty in that it is knowledge that a layman would be obliged to reveal, or in that the withholding of it from the public or from authorities compromises the integrity of the man who so withholds it, as in the case of the policeman who keeps connections with the underworld . . .[9]

This license to deviate, to ferret out secrets, and the resultant burden of guilty knowledge are the hallmarks of a profession.[10]

It is common practice for spokesmen at police ceremonial occasions to compare police work with a religious calling. It is apparent that there are many similarities between the role of the policeman and that of the priest, for example: an all-male society, a distinctive uniform, round-the-clock duty, a quasi-military regime, a code of ethics and strict regulation of conduct, the dual responsibility of controlling and serving the public, and finally the privilege of investigation and the acquisition of guilty knowledge.

Concomitant with the move toward professionalization in public relations and propaganda has been the effort within the police organization to improve quality and performance to meet the professional standards that have been established by a consensus of the experts. These are:

1. High standards of admission
2. A special body of knowledge and theory
3. Altruism and dedication to the service ideal

[9] Everett C. Hughes, "The Study of Occupations," in *Sociology Today*, eds. Robert K. Merton, Leonard Broom, and Leonard S. Cottrell, Jr. (New York: Basic Books Inc., 1959), p. 448.

[10] *Ibid.*, pp. 447–452.

4. A lengthy period of training for candidates
5. A code of ethics
6. Licensing of members
7. Autonomous control
8. Pride of the members in their profession
9. Publicly recognized status and prestige.[11]

The transformation from occupation to profession[12] has been compared heuristically to the sweep of a social movement.[13] Each stage of development must surmount the spe-

[11] See for example: A. M. Carr-Saunders and P. A. Wilson, "Professions," *Encyclopaedia of the Social Sciences* (New York: The Macmillan Co., 1935), Vol. 12, pp. 476-480; Henry P. Fairchild, ed. *Dictionary of Sociology* (New York: Philosophical Library, 1944), p. 235; Ernest Greenwood, "Attributes of a Profession," in *Man, Work, and Society*, eds. Sigmund Nosow and William H. Form (New York: Basic Books Inc., 1962), pp. 206-218; Robert C. Stone, "The Sociology of Bureaucracy and Professions," in *Contemporary Sociology*, ed. Joseph S. Roucek (New York: Philosophical Library, 1958), pp. 491-506; Talcott Parsons, "The Professions and Social Structure," *Social Forces*, Vol. 17 (May 1939), pp. 457-467; Morris L. Cogan, "The Problem of Defining a Profession," *The Annals of the American Academy of Political and Social Science*, Vol. 297 (1955), pp. 105-111; William J. Goode, "Encroachment, Charlatanism, and the Emerging Profession: Psychology, Sociology, and Medicine," *American Sociological Review*, Vol. 25 (December 1960), pp. 902-914.

[12] The number of professions and pseudo-professions seems to be constantly increasing. The New York State Educational Law, Title VIII, Article 131-151 recognizes such recent additions to the ranks of the professions as: nurses, pharmacists, accountants, surveyors, and shorthand reporters. Attempts have been made to professionalize the following occupations: Insurance Agents—Robert K. Bain, "The Process of Professionalization: Life Insurance Selling," (unpublished doctoral dissertation, University of Chicago, 1959); Real Estate Brokers—Everett C. Hughes, *Men and Their Work* (Glencoe: The Free Press, 1958), pp. 9, 44; Nuclear Technologists—Howard M. Vollmer and Donald L. Mills, "Nuclear Technology and the Professionalization of Labor," paper read before the American Sociological Association, New York City, August 31, 1960; Automobile Workers—Nelson N. Foote, "The Professionalization of Labor in Detroit," *American Journal of Sociology*, Vol. 58 (January 1953), pp. 371-380. For a list of other occupations moving in the direction of the professions and a criticism of their pretensions, see Harold L. Wilensky, "The Professionalization of Everyone?" *American Journal of Sociology*, Vol. 70 (September 1964), pp. 137-158.

[13] Rue Bucher and Anselm Strauss, "Professions in Process: An Emergent Approach," *American Journal of Sociology*, Vol. 66 (January 1961), pp. 325-334.

cial problems created by the broad shifts and innovations
in organizational structure, function, and ideology. To remain viable an emergent profession, like a revolutionary
government, must gain legitimation by the public. Then, in
order to protect itself from stagnation, it must make some
provision for the recruitment and advancement of "new
blood." A profession has to maintain its circulation of the
elite or it will be stricken with hardening of the hierarchies—
a chronic disease that finally atrophies the vital internal
organization.

Barriers to Professionalization

If the law-enforcement occupation is successful in obtaining the status of a profession, it will be a Horatio Alger
story. The great stumbling block is its traditionally low
status in our culture. A warped conception of policemen
has been cultivated in the mass media. The public holds
fast to the derogatory stereotypes of the grafting cop, the
sadistic cop, the dumb cop, the chiseling cop, and the thick-
brogued cop. There can be no profession where the public
refuses to grant high status and prestige. And it does not
help the police to call themselves "The Finest" as they do
in New York City. The title often backfires.

The low status of the police is almost *res adjudicata*.
For example, the Georgia courts have held that in certain
respects "the term policeman is the legal equivalent of 'watchman' at common law."[14] In the state of Michigan the court
has ruled several times that

[14] *Porter v. State,* 124 Georgia 297, 301 (1905).

The police force is nothing more, insofar as it is lawfully constituted, than an additional force of constables and watchmen appointed by the State for certain limited purposes.[15]

Sociological studies of occupational prestige point in the same direction. In 1947 the North-Hatt survey asked a representative national sample to evaluate the prestige of ninety occupations.[16] Policemen were ranked fifty-five, ten places below the midpoint. In 1963 a replication of that study placed the police occupation in the forty-seventh rank, just below the midpoint, an improvement of eight positions.[17] The coefficient of correlation between the results in the two surveys was .99. In sixteen years the occupational prestige ladder had not changed much.

The police occupation consistently maintains its rank below the midpoint of the scale in other countries as well. Table I shows the comparative standing as determined by similar surveys. In the fourth column the rank has been adjusted as if each were based upon a scale of one hundred occupations, and in interpreting these figures it should be kept in mind that the lower the number, the higher the rank.

When most people are asked to rank the police occupation, they immediately think of the patrolman on post who is the most visible representative of the police force. Thus the whole occupation, symbolized by the proletarian cop at the base of the occupational pyramid, is accorded the low prestige that is the lot of the working class in America.

15 *Allor v. Wayne County Auditors*, 43 Michigan 76, 98 (1880). This case was later cited approvingly as authority in *White v. Board of Supervisors of Manistee County*, 105 Michigan 608, 614 (1895).

16 Paul K. Hatt and C. C. North, "Prestige Ratings of Occupations," in *Man, Work, and Society*, eds. Sigmund Nosow and William H. Form (New York: Basic Books Inc., 1962), pp. 277–283.

17 Robert W. Hodge, Paul M. Siegel, and Peter H. Rossi, "Occupational Prestige in the United States, 1925–63," *American Journal of Sociology*, Vol. 70 (1964), p. 291.

TABLE I
OCCUPATIONAL RANK OF POLICEMEN[18]

(1) Country	(2) Rank in Original Scale	(3) Number of Occupations in Scale	(4) Comparative Rank Expressed as a Per Cent
United States (1963)	47	90	52
United States (1947)	55	90	61
Denmark	52	75	69
Japan	17	30	57
England	17	30	57
New Zealand	15	30	50
Australia	7	20	35

The status of police superior officers is altogether different. It is comparable to that of managerial executives in business corporations. And in actual practice, the public shows great respect for police officers. It seems logical that if there were an opportunity to make the distinction between subordinates and superiors, respondents would not lump all policemen together in the usual low rank, an effect observed in a Danish occupational survey.[19] To test this hypothesis I prepared a questionnaire that separated the various police ranks

---

[18] United States (1963)—Hodge, Siegel, and Rossi, *op. cit.*;
United States (1947)—Hatt and North, *op. cit.*;
Denmark—Kaare Svalastoga, *Prestige, Class, and Mobility* (Copenhagen: Gyldendal, 1959), p. 77;
Japan—Yoshiharu Scott Matsumoto, *Contemporary Japan: The Individual and the Group* (Philadelphia: American Philosophical Society, 1960), p. 37;
England—John Hall and D. Caradog Jones, "The Social Grading of Occupations," *British Journal of Sociology*, Vol. 1 (1950), pp. 31–55;
New Zealand—A. A. Congalton, "The Social Grading of Occupations in New Zealand," *British Journal of Sociology*, Vol. 4 (1953), pp. 45–59;
Australia—Ronald Taft, "The Social Grading of Occupations in Australia," *British Journal of Sociology*, Vol. 4 (1953), pp. 181–188.

[19] In the study by Svalastoga, *op. cit.*, policemen were ranked fifty-two out of a total of seventy-five occupations. In that same survey, chief of police was ranked fifteen.

among eighteen other occupations. In a pilot study sixty-five Queens College students (sophomores and juniors) were asked to rank the occupations according to the prestige they attached to each.

It is apparent from Table II that the results differed greatly from those obtained in the usual studies such as those reported in Table I. Police captain and lieutenant were placed in the top third of the twenty-three occupations, very close to the level of the professions.

TABLE II
How Queens College Students Ranked
Selected Occupations

N=65   1=Highest rank   23=Lowest rank

1. Doctor
2. Lawyer
3. Psychologist
4. Sociologist
5. Teacher
6. Accountant
7. FBI Agent
8. P.D. Captain
9. P.D. Lieutenant
10. Lieutenant, U.S. Army
11. P.D. Detective
12. P.D. Sergeant
13. Government Worker
14. Private Detective
15. Salesman
16. Carpenter
17. Patrolman
18. Farmer
19. Plumber
20. Auto Repairman
21. Clerk in a Store
22. Taxi Driver
23. Private, U.S. Army

The high rank of superior officers is significant in view of the results of a similar study by C. Douglas Gourley where there was a definite tendency for those of higher education (like college students) to rank policemen lower than did members of the public of lower educational background.[20]

Another powerful source of opposition to professionalization is the political machine, which traditionally seeks connections in the police force. When it gains influence, the machine demands favors for its followers. Whatever the ultimate effect may be on morale and morality, such alliances are profitable. Why should political bosses encourage the growth of a movement that automatically signifies the termination of the long-standing political partnership between the force and the politicians? Professionals are guided by universal, not particular criteria. Favoritism would be out; the politician would lose his influence.

One unusual obstacle to professionalization stems from the exhortations of its most enthusiastic proponents. The rank and file are staggered by the vast disparity between the reality of police work and this bombastic sermonizing, which reads like the beatitudes. Take, for example, the FBI code of ethics for American law-enforcement agents:

The FBI Pledge for Law Enforcement Officers

Humbly recognizing the responsibilities entrusted to me, I do vow that I shall always consider the high calling of law enforcement to be an honorable profession, the duties of which are recognized by me as both an art and a science. . . .

. . . .

I am aware of the serious responsibilities of my office and

[20] C. Douglas Gourley, *Public Relations and the Police* (Springfield: Charles C. Thomas, 1953), p. 102.

in the performance of my duties I shall, as a *minister*, seek
to supply comfort, advice and aid to those who may be
in need of such benefits; as a *soldier*, I shall wage vigorous
warfare against the enemies of my country, of its laws, and
of its principles; and as a *physician*, I shall seek to eliminate
the criminal parasite which preys upon our social order and
to strengthen the lawful processes of our body politic.

I shall strive to be both a *teacher* and a *pupil* in the art
and science of law enforcement. As a *lawyer*, I shall acquire
due knowledge of the laws of my domain and seek to
preserve and maintain the majesty and dignity of the law;
as a *scientist*, it will be my endeavor to learn all pertinent
truth about accusations and complaints which come to my
lawful knowledge; as an *artist*, I shall seek to use my skill
for the purpose of making each assignment a masterpiece;
as a *neighbor*, I shall bear an attitude of true friendship and
courteous respect to all citizens; and as an *officer*, I shall
always be loyal to my duty, my organization and my country. (Italics not in the original.)[21]

The scientist Norbert Wiener also eulogized the policeman
as hero:

The risk of being killed . . . is implicit and accepted, however, by every policeman. . . . These responsibilities are of
the same order as that of the early Christians in accepting
death in the arena rather than undergoing the disgrace and
humility of burning a pinch of incense before the Gods.[22]

When these saintly ideals and ethics are proposed as a
guide, the average policeman is apt to appraise their appeals
cynically. There are too many deviations from the codes
among the professionals themselves.

The patrolman on post can point out that as far as the

[21] United States Department of Justice, Federal Bureau of Investigation
National Academy, *The FBI Pledge for Law Enforcement Officers* (Washington: Federal Bureau of Investigation National Academy, 1959).

[22] Norbert Wiener, "The Grand Privilege: A Scholar's Appreciation,"
Saturday Review, Vol. 43 (March 5, 1960), p. 54.

risk of being killed goes, it is he who takes it most often. The professional officer, because of his higher rank or special assignment, is more likely to be doing paper work in an office than to be patrolling the streets of a crime-ridden section of the city. The many policemen who have been threatened with complaints by superior officers for unnecessary conversation (which is a violation of police rules) scoff at the idea of acting in the capacity of minister, teacher, or lawyer. Merely talking to members of the public is discouraged.

The man on post wonders if the idealists were ever patrolmen themselves. Finding it impossible to live up to such a code, he is inclined to ignore it altogether, and rationalize his guilt feelings by disparaging both the code and the men behind it. Some professionals leave themselves open to such attack by attending college classes while they are supposed to be working. Others "acquire religion" only after promotion, when they are protected from the dangers and temptations of the men out on patrol.

Thus the codes of ethics and ideals that are not consistent with the force's sense of reality may actually impede professionalization. For example, professionals advocate higher education for policemen, to whom school represents at best a waste of time. Professionals support respect for the civil rights of minority groups, which the average policeman considers a concession to "the other side." Professionals want policemen to be active and involved in their duties, whereas many patrolmen are content to drift along doing as little as possible. These members of the force feel threatened by the proposed changes. In self-defense they join the opposition to professionalism and become part of the subculture of cynicism.

Consequences of Professionalization

As their campaign has gained momentum, the propagandists have advanced from the idea that professionalism ought to be achieved to the conviction (on paper at least) that it has already been. Although this still has to be validated by public opinion, leaders of the movement are extending themselves to make it true.

In attempting to carve out a specialty, the leading theoreticians face a situation comparable to that of the early sociologists. Police Science, at best, is a synthetic subject that has borrowed heavily from several well-established disciplines: public administration, the legal profession (with which it shares criminal law), sociology, psychology, psychoanalysis, and human relations. A "professional" police organization's administrators must be familiar with the fundamentals of behavioral and organizational theory. Thus the quest for professionalization has forced attendance at interdisciplinary conferences on race relations, crime and delinquency, and community problems. Inexorably, the social-science orientation, its ethic based on human dignity, has invaded the police system. As a result, the professionals have spread a police doctrine of decreased emphasis upon the use of force, so dramatic a departure from the traditional "lock-them-up" philosophy that in 1957 George E. Sokolsky devoted a column to it, entitled "Our New Style Cop on the Beat."

> The new style policeman needs to know law and accounting and languages and in our polyglot big cities some history and sociology. . . . Thus, a police officer who is also a sociologist and has done special work in minority groups is an asset.

The old-fashioned idea of a cop with a club who splits
a skull to put down street fights is of no value today. . . .

So conscious have the police become of the vagaries of the
law and the anxieties of the higher courts that the criminal's
constitutional rights be protected that those who are given
this academic instruction in New York are given courses
in: The Constitution and Due Process; The Courts; Criminal
Law and Modus Operandi; Municipal Law; Evidence.

Presumably similar courses are given in other cities where
such academies have been organized. One effect of all this
could be so to inhibit the policeman that he would be afraid
to arrest anyone.[23]

Along with the shift from the ideal of the tough cop to
that of the social-scientist police officer has gone a parallel
shift within the organization from the authoritarian pattern
of discipline under which patrolmen trembled, to a less punitive one. Techniques of persuasion, manipulation, and conference are now the rule.

In public relations the results of this new orientation have
been even more dramatic. The modern police force stresses
service to the community; solicits the cooperation of the
public; encourages guided tours of police buildings. In
Chicago the headquarters police "live in glass houses" so
that the public can see them in operation.[24] In New York
City the department has established civilian liaison committees
to help promote better relations with the Negro and Puerto
Rican communities.[25] Even attitudes toward criminals have
been somewhat softened in metropolitan police forces. Policemen are learning to comply with legal restrictions on their
right to arrest, search, seize, and interrogate.

[23] New York *Journal American*, June 12, 1957, p. 26. See also the series
of articles by Robert S. Bird, "Cops or Social Scientists," New York *Herald
Tribune*, July 10, July 17, July 24, 1960.

[24] O. W. Wilson, "How the Police Chief Sees It," *Harper's*, Vol. 228
(April 1964), p. 141.

[25] New York *Times*, March 29, 1965, p. 35.

Emile Durkheim's classic distinction between organic and mechanical solidarity in a social system[26] may illuminate this radical departure from time-honored police ideology. According to Durkheim, primitive and less complex societies are bound together by bonds of mechanical solidarity based on resemblance and custom, while more advanced social systems generate a qualitatively different type of organic solidarity growing out of the division of labor. It is possible to compare the two types by studying the society's law, the external symbol of solidarity.[27] As society progresses toward what we moderns complacently call higher civilization, law becomes restitutive rather than repressive. Repressive law is preeminently penal law in its punitive vengeful aspect—the *lex talionis*. Restitutive law on the other hand aims primarily to restore the status quo rather than to punish.[28]

The application of this concept to police work leads to some intriguing analogies. The modern metropolitan department, complex and highly specialized in its division of labor, is the counterpart of the organically integrated society. The traditional police force, such as previously existed in American cities and still does in smaller communities, more primitive, stable, conservative, and "reliable" than the contemporary urban police organization, is bound by mechanical solidarity. If the comparison is valid, then rural police forces today should be the most punitive and repressive; large urban departments, the most humane and most involved in civil and administrative functions; and police in small cities somewhere between these two extremes.

[26] Emile Durkheim, *The Division of Labor in Society* (Glencoe: The Free Press, 1965).

[27] *Ibid.*, p. 64.

[28] *Ibid.*, p. 69. For a provocative study that contradicts Durkheim's theory of the progression from repressive to restitutive legal institutions, see Richard D. Schwartz and James C. Miller, "Legal Evolution and Societal Complexity," *American Journal of Sociology*, Vol. 70 (September 1964), p. 166.

A good indication of police ideology is the percentage of cases cleared by arrest. The tougher the ideology, the larger the percentage of arrests. If the outlook is less punitive, there will be fuller preliminary investigations before an arrest is officially made, and when the case is weak, or evidence is uncovered leading to a presumption of innocence, the suspect will not be arrested. Furthermore, a concern for civil rights will prevent the use of forced confessions or other illegally obtained evidence.

The percentage of arrests made, when computed from the total number of offenses known, therefore, provides a rough estimate of just how punitive and repressive a police force is. The FBI Crime Reports disclose that from 1960–1965 the police departments in rural areas, and in cities with a population under ten thousand, had a higher rate of arrest for each year than any of the groups of cities with larger populations. In every year but one (1960), the rate of arrest in rural areas was higher than that in the small cities.[29]

The solidarity of the large metropolitan department is, however, somewhat weakened by the powerful advocates of professionalization who insist that all policemen ought to be well educated. Superior officers who want promotion are almost forced to register for college courses in human relations[30] and executive development; and a good proportion of patrolmen take courses in their spare time. In New York City, the culmination of these efforts was the creation of a police college in June 1964 that became part of the City University.

[29] *FBI Uniform Crime Reports*, 1960, 1961, 1962, 1963, 1964, 1965, Table 8.
[30] When promotion comes, these college credits are publicized. For example, for a recently promoted assistant chief inspector, the press release stated that "The new appointee . . . has studied sociology and police administration at Manhattan College, New York University, and the Baruch School. . . ." See New York *Times*, November 9, 1965, p. 37.

The police elite's enthusiasm for the benefits of education has obscured for them its negative effects: the envy and hostility it is spreading among the old-timers who lack the formal education to meet the proposed standards,[31] and among the police students who, sometimes for twenty years, try to graduate from the cram schools and gain promotion. This division along educational lines is most clearly revealed when a member of the force with little education succeeds in being promoted. Thenceforth he loses no opportunity to impress on his college-trained subordinates the fact that he is their boss, though he never graduated from elementary school.

The professional spirit also stimulates competition for promotion, but only one out of every ten patrolmen who take the test for sergeant makes it. Ghoulish jesters who hang rope nooses on the lockers of the failing candidates in no way alleviate the frustration of those who were touted as "sure things" before the test. A few of the unsuccessful have nervous breakdowns; far more transfer their allegiance from the professionally oriented groups to the hard-core cynics.

Nevertheless, professionalization is a wonderful tonic for the police occupation because it brings to an institution in transition the enthusiasm, pride, and ideals it needs to rebuild.[32] But the erection of a new structure on old founda-

[31] Almost two-thirds of the sample in the cynicism study were against requiring a college degree for admission to the force (see Appendix).

[32] On the purely administrative level the goal of those in favor of professionalization is to carry the bureaucratization of the police to its highest degree although they would belligerently deny this interpretation. They want those advantages in scientific administration that Max Weber has described as the fruit of the fully developed bureaucratic mechanism: "Precision, speed, unambiguity, knowledge of the files, continuity, discretion, unity, strict subordination, reduction of friction, and of material and personal costs—these are raised to the optimum point in the strictly bureaucratic administration. . . ." Gerth and Mills, *op. cit.*, p. 214.

tions necessarily produces strains and weak spots. Although the social relations between ranks, especially between sergeant and patrolman, have improved, the split in the department along the lines of professionalization and education has created a new and more abrasive type of social tension.

CHAPTER 2

Becoming a Policeman

The Selection Process

In order to qualify for appointment to a modern urban police force, the candidate must successfully thread his way through a series of rigorous requirements, some of which do not necessarily provide exactly the person the modern police force needs.

The first hurdle is the written examination,[1] which has become a modified intelligence test. During the last ten years the average I.Q. for a class of recruits at the New York City Police Academy has been approximately 105. This means that anyone with an I.Q. below the normal range has small chance of being appointed, and the same is true in the other major police forces, which was not the case in the past.[2]

About fifty per cent of the applicants who pass the examination are subsequently eliminated by the character investiga-

[1] After passing the written test the police applicant must meet the following typical standards: 1. U.S. citizenship, 2. Minimum age of twenty-one years, 3. Fingerprinting of applicants, 4. No record of felony offense connection, 5. Good moral character determined by a complete background-check investigation, 6. Education through 12th grade, 7. Good physical fitness as shown by a complete medical examination, 8. Successful passing of an oral interview examination by the hiring agency. See Gene S. Muehleisen, "Standards and Training for Peace Officers," *FBI Law Enforcement Bulletin*, Vol. 34 (March 1965), p. 12.

[2] See earlier references to the low level of intelligence found in police candidates and policemen in Terman *et al.*, *op. cit.* and Bain, *op. cit.*

tion, which turns up something unfavorable in their past record. Knowing this, some sophisticated candidates begin their adjustment to the demands of their new career immediately after they are notified that they have passed the written examination. In anticipation of a visit by a police department investigator whose guiding principle is, "Any and every doubt must be resolved in favor of the department," they dispose of books that might be considered too radical and drop friends with unsavory reputations.

The doctrines of *ex post facto* responsibility and guilt by association are used to establish a case against an applicant, and there is little chance of redress. The person who successfully survives this ordeal is "clean as a hound's tooth" (a rather notorious compliment). In 1964 former Commissioner Michael Murphy, reviewing the screening procedures, observed that

> Today's policeman is younger, better trained, and more carefully screened than ever before. We investigate candidates from the time they were in Kindergarten to their entrance in the department. The report on every one of them runs from 60 to 75 pages of material.[3]

The police department unit responsible for the investigation of applicants is making approval increasingly difficult for candidates. In one case, a misstep by a boy of thirteen, a mere delinquency, barred him from a police appointment, even though he had lived an exemplary life for more than fifteen years thereafter. He, however, successfully petitioned the New York State Supreme Court to compel the Police Commissioner to appoint him in spite of his youthful peccadillo.[4]

Many departments also subject applicants to psychiatric examinations, using Rorschach and Minnesota Multiphasic

[3] New York *Times*, February 23, 1964, p. 45.
[4] New York *Times*, February 9, 1961, p. 22.

profiles to aid evaluation.[5] The truly "progressive" professional administrator adds to this battery a session with
the Deceptograph (lie detector) in which the hopeful aspirant
pits his wits against the machine.[6] One police captain described the value of the polygraph as

> the ability to detect the attempts at deception and to un-
> cover a multitude of undetected crimes such as thievery,
> homosexuality, emotional instability, and attempts to hide
> physical disabilities or ailments and any omissions and false
> statements made on the official police questionnaire.[7]

Frequently, idealistic youngsters sign petitions or join
liberal organizations in the hope of ameliorating social conditions. It follows that police departments who classify them
as poor risks are disqualifying some candidates who would
capably fulfill the professional requirement of dedication to
the service of the public.

As a result of all these procedures very few applicants are
actually appointed to the force. In New York City the rate
of acceptance has remained close to fifteen per cent for
many years.[8] Tucson, Arizona, reported several years ago
a rate of six per cent.[9] From 1950 to 1962 in Los Angeles it

[5] James H. Rankin, "Psychiatric Screening of Police Recruits," *Public
Personnel Review*, Vol. 20 (July 1959), pp. 191–196.

[6] Captain Paul H. Bohardt, "Tucson Uses New Police Personnel Selection Methods," *FBI Law Enforcement Bulletin*, Vol. 28 (September, 1959),
pp. 8–12.

[7] *Ibid.*, p. 11; To the same effect see Chris Gugas, "Better Policemen
Through Better Screening," *Police*, Vol. 6 (July–August 1962), pp. 54–58, in
which it is alleged that thirty-five police departments are now using the
polygraph as part of the personnel selection program.

[8] Leo Eilbert, John McNamara, and Vernon Hanson, *Research on Selection and Training for Police Recruits: First Annual Report* (New York:
American Institute for Research, 1961), p. 6, and also personal conversations
with members of the Police Academy Investigation Unit. Former Commissioner Michael Murphy places the figure at 8⅓ per cent. He estimated that
one of every twelve applicants was accepted. See Michael J. Murphy, "Improving the Law Enforcement Image," *Journal of Criminal Law, Criminology and Police Science*, Vol. 56 (March 1965), p. 107.

[9] Paul H. Bohardt, *op. cit.*, p. 12.

was only four per cent.[10] Other jurisdictions are almost equally strict.[11]

This raises the question of how, and from which groups in the society, the police continue to fill their ranks. Despite the obvious appeal of adventure and the military milieu for many young men, there is ample evidence that security is the foremost lure for the typical candidate. Thousands of recruits at the New York Police Academy have been asked why they joined the force. The overwhelming majority indicated that they wanted the security it offered.[12] It is further apparent that this lure is strongest among the working class who view a police career as a step upward in the social scale. (Perhaps one of the reasons police work represents downward mobility for a middle-class individual in the United States is that the policeman must commit himself to the use of force, on which middle-class morality frowns.)

For the past fifteen years, during a cycle of prosperity, the bulk of police candidates has been upper lower class with a sprinkling of lower middle class; about ninety-five per cent has had no college training. This was substantiated by a survey of the backgrounds of more than 1,200 recruits who graduated from the New York Police Academy. The occupations of the recruits' fathers were classified according to the *Dictionary of Occupational Titles*. The results appear in Table III.

[10] *The Police: An Interview by Donald McDonald with William H. Parker, Chief of Police of Los Angeles* (Santa Barbara: Center for the Study of Democratic Institutions, 1962), p. 11.

[11] Portland, Oregon, had a success rate of six per cent from 1959 through 1962. See Joseph D. Matarazzo, *et al.*, "Characteristics of Successful Policemen and Firemen Applicants," *Journal of Applied Psychology*, Vol. 48 (1964), pp. 123–133. The Berkeley, California, force appoints about five per cent of the applicants. See David Wilson, "Psychiatric Evaluation in the Selection Process," in *Police Selection*, ed. Richard H. Blum (Springfield: Charles C. Thomas, 1964), p. 152.

[12] For a fuller discussion of their motivation for joining the force, see Chapter 5.

TABLE III
OCCUPATIONS OF FATHERS OF RECRUITS
(N=1,214)

Type of Occupation	Number of Fathers	Per Cent of Total
Professional	28	2.3
Semi-Professional	7	.6
Proprietors	49	4.2
Managers and Supervisors	72	6.0
Clerical	76	6.3
Sales	30	2.5
Protective Service	132	11.0
Skilled Workers	311	25.6
Semi-Skilled Workers	237	19.0
Unskilled Workers	96	8.0
Service (Not Protective)	160	13.2
Farm and Kindred Workers	16	1.3
Totals	1,214	100

From the category of Clerical Workers through Farm Workers, the occupations are compatible with working-class membership, and they make up more than eighty-five per cent of the total. It is interesting to note that eighty-four fathers (seven per cent) were policemen[13] and that twenty-three (two per cent) were firemen.

From a practical point of view, the working-class youth may develop into a more dependable policeman than the middle-class college student, simply because he has already been tested in a gang and street-corner society. If he has remained out of trouble until he is eligible for the appointment, he is a good risk,[14] and his behavior under the stress of

[13] In a study of a small Midwestern police force the investigator found that seventy per cent of the policemen interviewed did not want their sons to become policemen. See William A. Westley, "The Police: A Sociological Study of Law, Custom, and Morality," *op. cit.*, p. 235.

[14] During the period 1959 through 1962 in Portland, Oregon, 116 men were appointed to the force. Most were from the lower socio-economic classes. No more than three per cent were college graduates. Yet after an exhaustive psychological study of the 116 successful candidates, the conclusion emerged that they were above average in emotional stability and

police emergencies will probably conform closely to traditional police expectations. Although the college-trained applicant is more likely to possess an unblemished past, he has been insulated to a great extent from the trials of the social arena. As such, he is an unknown quantity: it is impossible to predict how he will react to the pressure and strain inherent in police life. Because of his educational advantage, he is the police superior of the future,[15] but because of his untested nature, he will introduce an element of uncertainty into the ruling ranks of the force.

The end result of the process of elimination is to accentuate the medium and mediocre at the expense of the independent and exceptional. Working-class background, high-school education or less, average intelligence, cautious personality—these are the typical features of the modern police recruit. Only in his superior physical endowment does he stand above the crowd.

The professionals are, of course, making every effort to reach the college student and convince him of the virtues of a police career in order to ensure future control of the force by a professional elite. At present there is a precarious balance of power, but unless a steady stream of middle-class, college-trained men become policemen, the professionals will

intelligence (I.Q. averaged 112), and that they were superior young men. See Joseph D. Matarazzo, *et al.*, "Characteristics of Successful Policemen and Firemen Applicants," *Journal of Applied Psychology*, Vol. 48 (1964), pp. 123–133.

[15] In 1963 roughly four per cent of the New York force were college graduates, and fourteen per cent of the superior officers were college graduates. The concentration of college graduates among superiors is three times the rate among the force as a whole. Of every ten college graduates, four will become superiors, whereas one in ten men who do not have college degrees will be promoted. See Gerald M. Leonard, "The Undergraduate Police Science Program and Its Relationship with the New York Police Department" (unpublished Master's thesis, Bernard M. Baruch School of Business and Public Administration, The City College of the City University of New York, 1964), pp. 57–61.

have to struggle desperately to maintain their influence among lower-class policemen who do not respond favorably to the professional ideology.

In the face of this looming defeat[16] the professionals have hurled a challenge:

> Let us think big! Let us demand a minimum of four years of college with a Bachelor of Science Degree in Law Enforcement.[17]

To implement this call for education, they have inaugurated cadet and apprentice programs to interest possible college entrants in police work. The students are put to work in police offices with their hours arranged to permit them to attend their college courses, in the hope that if an apprentice gets a taste of police work before his more mature judgment impels him toward an occupation with higher status, he will be satisfied with a career in law enforcement.

At the same time the drive for professionalism has led to a compulsive and unwarranted dependence upon the selection process. Dedicated to the proposition that law enforcement is a noble calling, especially since it has been subjected to the

[16] How unpromising the prospects are can be seen from an examination of the figures. In New York City the police have been campaigning strenuously for many years to recruit college men. But in the ten year period, 1953–1963, of nearly 15,000 new policemen appointed, only 320 (just over two per cent) were college graduates. See Leonard, *op. cit.*, p. 68. The Los Angeles department has also concentrated its attention upon the college graduate. Its percentage of college graduates is a little higher than that of other major police forces. Of 5,000 members of the force, 280 (5.6%) are holders of college degrees. See Samuel H. Jameson, "Controversial Areas in 20th Century Policing," in *Interdisciplinary Problems in Criminology: Papers of the American Society of Criminology*, 1964, eds. Walter C. Reckless and Charles L. Newman (Columbus: The College of Commerce and Administration, The Ohio State University, 1965), p. 129.

[17] Carroll S. Price, "Police Prestige—Hopeless?" *Police*, Vol. 6 (September–October 1961), p. 40. A similar thought is expressed by Quinn Tamm, Executive Director of the International Association of Chiefs of Police, "The college campus must be looked to for the police officers of the future." See New York *Daily News*, November 11, 1965, p. 59.

prophylactic operation of his own professional administration and code of ethics, the would-be professional cannot bring himself to blame the police system for the endemic evils it has spawned, but insists that the fault lies in the individual. His solution, then, is to obtain better men. The best method, in his opinion, is to tighten up the selection process: to raise admission standards, add more psychiatric and lie detector tests, make more stringent an already cumbersome background investigation.

Unfortunately, these ingenious devices are self-defeating. The future recruit may have a year or two more of college, and there may be no kurtosis of his personality profile. He may be a trifle larger and stronger, his eyes may need one diopter less of correction, and three additional character references may swell the bursting covers of his investigator's portfolio. But in the important qualities he will turn out to be closer to the average, and more conforming, than ever before. No new variable will have been introduced to upset the customary pattern of the police career.

Where is the real source of trouble? Can all failures be exorcised by criticizing the selection process? Or does the cause lie in the police system itself? To unravel the mystery of what goes wrong, it is necessary to trace the recruit's career, starting with the training period.

The Rookie at the Police Academy

The cord binding the rookie to the civilian world is clipped at the Police Academy, where the beginner is taught the fundamentals of his job. But the deeper significance of the training period is that the Police Academy is, to use Erving

Goffman's phrase, a "total institution" which "strips and mortifies" the recruit.

> First, to a degree, authority is of the echelon kind. Any member of the staff class has certain rights to discipline any member of the inmate class. . . .
>
> Second, the authority of corrective sanctions is directed to a great multitude of items of conduct of the kind that are constantly coming up for judgment; in brief, authority is directed to matters of dress, deportment, social intercourse, manners, and the like. . . .
>
> The third feature of authority in total institutions is that misbehaviors in one sphere of life are held against one's standing in other spheres.[18]

The stripping and mortification accelerate rapidly. Each neophyte proudly, albeit nervously, accepts the visible insignia of his new office: uniform, revolver, nightstick, and shield. Each of these symbols entails a continuous responsibility, which constantly reminds the recruit of his new role— a role that soon comes to dominate his personality.

In the beginning he faces a world in which he is always out of step. The simplest task becomes cause for anxiety. He must learn even such fundamental activities as breathing and walking all over again.[19] The routine of dressing proves to be a complicated puzzle, with daily inspections to reinforce his anxiety. Buttons, snaps, belts, and fasteners require special techniques. Securing the shield appropriately by a huge safety pin demands dexterity of touch. Even going to the toilet is a ritual. The rules dictate the formula by which the patrolman must request permission from a superior officer to leave post

---

[18] Erving Goffman, "Characteristics of Total Institutions," in *Identity and Anxiety*, ed. Maurice Stein, *et al.* (Glencoe: The Free Press, 1960), p. 455.

[19] Quentin Reynolds, *Headquarters* (New York: Popular Library, 1956), pp. 26–27.

for "personal necessity." Any substantial departure from this will probably bring a complaint and fine.

The tools of the police trade are lethal. Until he gains complete control of revolver and nightstick, the rookie is more of a menace to the public than a protector. Proper position, efficient handling, and safety precautions are drilled into him during interminable sessions of practice, and in spite of this, station houses and private residences still bear scars and holes from stray bullets accidentally fired by police novices.

These weapons fascinate the new owner. Their symbolic significance is obvious even to those who usually scoff at Freudian interpretations and may explain the time and concentration the rookie lavishes on the nightstick. The recruit loves to twirl his baton, but this treacherous instrument will not be easily subdued. It strikes back by wounding its master's most sensitive spots. The department might be wise to recommend that recruits wear knee guards and the aluminum cup protectors used by prizefighters.

For two months the recruit at the Academy is cut off from the rest of the department and overwhelmed by a mountain of study, most of it complex and demanding. The curriculum is broken down into academic divisions: law, government, police procedures and techniques, police in the community, human relations, rules and regulations. In his spare time there is physical training: judo, first aid, and shooting practice.

At the Academy he masters, and simultaneously succumbs to, the web of protocol and ceremony that characterizes any quasi-military hierarchy. This formality serves as a blueprint for interaction and performs the vital task of binding the various ranks into a smoothly functioning unit, while at the same time maintaining the distinction among hierarchical levels. Structure is built into situations, roles are indicated, interpersonal difficulties are smoothed over—all by a snappy salute or click of the heels. Critics sometimes charge that these exaggerated patterns of deference are anachronisms from an aristocratic society and unsuited to our democratic egalitarian nation. Yet, one must admit that on a more subdued scale etiquette plays a role in our civilian culture similar to its function in the police force.[20]

At the Academy the recruit also absorbs many lessons not included in the official curriculum. Through contact with his instructor he subconsciously acquires the technique that lends artistry to police work—an instinct for the proper time to be masterly or to genuflect, to be warm and sympathetic or cold and imperious toward his future clientele.

The typical police recruit starts his career without a trace of cynicism,[21] but after a short time at the Academy, the alert student begins to realize that the professional atmosphere that surrounds him is partly a sham. This intuition may arise from the innuendos of his instructor; more often it is the result of the demeaning restrictions imposed upon his private life. In class he is taught that his exalted status as a policeman and peace officer endows him with tremendous power and responsibility. Outside of class the department indicates in many ways that it does not trust the young probationer. It sets a curfew for him; it declares stores where liquor is sold "off-limits." The recruit measures this treat-

[20] See Robert Bierstedt, *The Social Order* (New York: McGraw-Hill Book Company, Inc., 1963), pp. 253–254.

[21] In the cynicism study described in the Appendix, thirty-four newly appointed probationary patrolmen were chosen as the control group and given questionnaires to fill out on their first day at the police training school. Only one of them revealed any hint of cynicism. By contrast forty-five per cent of the respondents with two or three months of experience at the Academy were included among those high on the cynicism scale. It should be noted, however, that cynicism at this stage of the career is probably only a spurious affectation of sophistication to conceal insecurity and naïveté.

ment against the frequent appeals to him to conduct himself like a professional. Doubts assail him.

The Academy curriculum stresses ethics, ideals, and professionalism. This introduces a striking disparity between class lectures and the conditions of police patrol out on the streets, which the lower-class recruit knows from firsthand experience; a month or two before, he was a member of the lower-class public, critically assessing policemen. He begins to question the truth of the instructor's words.

When the recruit finally meets older members of the force, he is introduced to another source of cynicism. The more experienced men tell him that in order to become a real policeman, he will have to forget everything he is learning at the Academy.

Other occupations and professions are, of course, faced with the same problem of disillusionment. The experience of freshman medical students, for example, parallels that of the police recruit.

> The medical students enter school with what we may think of as the idealistic notion, implicit in lay culture, that the practice of medicine is a wonderful thing and that they are going to devote their lives to service to mankind. . . . In several ways the first year of medical school does not live up to their expectations. They are disillusioned. . . . They come to think that their courses . . . are not worth much . . . and, in the second place, the subject matter itself is irrelevant.[22]

However, the student physicians' loss of idealism is, according to Howard S. Becker and Blanche Geer, only temporary, restricted to the first year at medical school.

[22] Howard S. Becker and Blanche Geer, "The Fate of Idealism in Medical School," *American Sociological Review*, Vol. 23 (February 1958), p. 51.

Cynicism, griping, and minor cheating become endemic, but the cynicism is specific to the educational situation, to the first year, and to only parts of it. Thus the students keep their cynicism separate from their idealistic feelings and by postponement protect their belief that medicine is a wonderful thing, that their school is a fine one, and that they will become good doctors.[23]

Cynicism in the freshman policeman may also be temporary, but often becomes a permanent pattern of response, particularly when the newcomer enters with a strong sense of idealism and inevitably encounters situations where failure and frustration overwhelm him.

The Police Academy Instructor

The Police Academy instructor, a father figure for hundreds of future patrolmen, serves as a kind of therapist in uniform and deserves special attention. He not only teaches his students in the classroom, he patrols with them on their practice tours, becoming the role-model on the job. Often a father confessor to confused beginners, he is nevertheless far from permissive: he expects complete and immediate obedience as he relentlessly spells out each item of the blueprint that the class must internalize.

The police instructor is usually an experienced superior officer with a college degree, whose record is as nearly spotless as possible. Before his assignment to this sensitive post, the police-department equivalent of a college dean of faculty has carefully evaluated confidential reports and recommendations on him. Various factors precipitate police intellectuals and professionals into the training and staff divi-

[23] *Ibid.*, pp. 52–53.

sion. The first is the leadership's desire to prove to the world that the "dumb cop" is a relic of the past. The second is the resistance of line organizations and vested interests to disturbing influences. The practical policeman, in particular the typical field commander, rightly believes that in active police work intellectuals and professionally oriented men disrupt traditional work patterns, which in practice depart on many counts from the ideal, officially recommended procedure.

The future instructor on his part is frequently happy to get away from the temptations and heartaches that are unavoidable for members of the patrol force. By the time he has had enough experience to be considered for an instructorship, police work has probably lost whatever thrill it once had, and he is ready to welcome a sojourn in the "ivory tower" where he is safe from trouble. His motivation is similar to that of lawyers competing for judgeships, who, according to David Riesman, find something "in law practice, even in the most refined offices, which is felt as dirty work, from which the bench is an escape."[24]

For once the "pros and cons" of the situation all point in the same direction. It is to the interest of all concerned to see college graduates, the idealistic, professionally oriented members of the force, assigned to the Police Academy. But even while the new instructor is congratulating himself, a residue of guilt simmers in his heart because he has left the firing line. Every instructor in a department that considers itself professional is the victim of a role conflict. His self-conception often fights with his teaching function. He must decide whether he sees himself as primarily an academician (a college professor), or as an experienced practical policeman who is

[24] David Riesman, "Toward an Anthropological Science of Law and the Legal Profession," in *Individualism Reconsidered and Other Essays* (Glencoe: The Free Press, 1954), p. 442.

using academic techniques only secondarily to impart a working knowledge of the job to the new men. The two roles can rarely be successfully combined.

This nerve-wracking confusion of identity constantly crops up to plague the police instructor. He would like to imagine himself a superior "new breed" of policeman who has been chosen for his charismatic quality. Instead, he is relegated to a peculiar interstitial niche by his former colleagues in the field who constantly accuse him of having lost touch with the reality of police work in the street. Even more rankling than this loss of face is the insinuation that he is doing a poor job of teaching because the recruit has to learn police work all over again when he is transferred from the cloistered halls of the Academy to his precinct field assignment. His students are not above asking with malicious ingenuousness, "Lieutenant, were you ever out on patrol, or have you always been assigned to the Academy?" And the "oft-repeated judgment of graduates that attendance at the recruit school represents 'just a waste of time' "[25] sinks the barb still deeper.

Finally there is the challenge to his academic competence posed by the few college graduates who may be students in his class. To counter this he delivers many lectures deprecating the difficulty of college courses in comparison to the police-science curriculum at the Academy.

But beyond all these external irritations and conflicts, the instructor faces the central issue of determining what the final aim of his course ought to be. Should he teach the student to function as an ideal type—to act in accordance with professional standards? Or should he prepare him for the practical approach of the precinct? If the instructor views the police society as needing rehabilitation, he will teach the

[25] Bruce Smith, *The New York Police Survey* (New York: Institute of Public Administration, 1952), p. 5.

ideal *modus operandi*. In this way through each pupil who graduates, he indirectly gives the system a nudge in the right direction. But if he lowers his sights and, like many therapists, is willing to settle for life adjustment, he will teach a practical course that will make it easy for the student to find a comfortable spot in the precinct milieu—and that will also perpetuate the old style with all its defects. Usually, however, the instructor reaches a compromise: his class lectures oscillate between appeals to universal criteria of conduct and admissions that, in practice, the police force operates not *sub specie aeternitatis*, but in a very pragmatic, opportunistic fashion.

Reality Shock

"Freshmen" always accept the initial period of training with enthusiasm. The first portent of trouble appears when recruits are sent several times a week from the Academy to the precincts for seasoning in the field. The practice in most departments is to assign an experienced patrolman to accompany the rookie. In New York City, the professional Academy environment is reproduced as closely as possible on the streets. The class is split into teams of two, and each pair is assigned to patrol a post under the supervision of the Academy instructor. Officially, this procedure is justified as a pedagogical method of maintaining continuity between theory and practice. Unofficially, its purpose is to shield the student policemen from "contagion" by other patrolmen in the precinct. But since the instructor cannot be everywhere at once, his "charges" have ample opportunity to communicate with veterans on the beat and get a taste of real police work "on their own."

From this point on the whole attitude of the class changes. The pupils show less interest in study. Examination marks fall. Sociologists have very appropriately characterized such a syndrome, which is also common to the professions of social work,[26] teaching, medicine, and law, as "reality shock." The essence of the shock is the demoralizing realization of the vast discrepancy between idealistic expectations and sordid reality. William Westley argues that for the young policeman the critical variable in reality shock is the contact with the hostile and unappreciative public to which the patrolman reacts by increasing his solidarity with the force.[27] This may be true, but reality shock may also lead to disenchantment with the occupation itself, and this double-edged effect has not been emphasized enough. Beyond this, the shock may be caused not so much by the public as by the intimate knowledge of the job itself. In the case of the policeman, this may be, on a superficial level, the horror of handling one's first "ripe D.O.A." (a dead body that has decomposed after several days in the heat of the summer) or the difficulty of adjusting to a set of "late tours" (duty from 12 Midnight to 8:00 A.M.). On a deeper level, it is growing disenchantment with the police system.

The rookie begins with faith in the system. He tries to follow the book of rules and regulations. Then, he discovers that many cases have repercussions of which the book seems

[26] See Lloyd E. Ohlin, H. Piven, and Don Pappenfort, "Major Dilemmas of the Social Worker in Probation and Parole," *National Probation and Parole Association*, Vol. 2 (July 1956), p. 222. A recent study of low-income families was strongly critical of the "condescension and contempt of many social workers toward the poor." New York *Times*, February 20, 1966, p. 42. For an analysis of reality shock among correctional personnel on the staff of an institution for delinquents, see Charles Perrow, "Reality Shock: A New Organization Confronts the Custody-Treatment Dilemma," *Social Problems*, Vol. 10 (Spring 1963), pp. 374–382.

[27] William A. Westley, "The Police: A Sociological Study of Law, Custom, and Morality," *op. cit.*, pp. 256, 282.

wholly ignorant. He is chastised by his colleagues for being naïve enough to follow the book. Gradually he learns to neglect the formal rules and norms and turns elsewhere for direction. Individual interpretation replaces the formal authoritative dictum of the official book and the young policeman is an easy prey to cynicism. This may not be typical of every police career, but it happens frequently enough to constitute a serious problem.

Occasionally reality shock is converted into a constructive experience that exhilarates the recruit and builds up his enthusiasm for police duty. One incident will serve as a vivid example of how powerfully a rookie's outlook may be molded by his early contacts with the public. Assigned from the Police Academy to a patrol precinct, a recruit was performing a practice tour of duty under the watchful supervision of his Academy instructor. When he signaled the station house over the police call box, he was directed to proceed to a location in a tenement area to handle an aided case. (An aided case in police terminology means that someone is sick or injured, and that an ambulance is responding.)

This time it was a maternity case. It is always thrilling for a policeman to assist at a delivery. There is the possibility that the child will be named after him, and the probability of favorable publicity in the newspapers. Imbued with this "professional" motivation, the rookie opened the door to find the pregnant woman in bed, being cared for by a good-looking friend.

As the young policeman led them down the dark and chilly stairs toward the ambulance, the nobly proportioned friend unbuttoned her sweater and wrapped it around the shoulders of the expectant mother. The rookie could only stare in admiration. The friend had nothing on underneath the sweater. It is safe to predict every future aided case will bring an anticipatory glow to this policeman and recall pleasant memories.

Most duties are less glamorous; some leave a bitter taste. Because the recruit at the Academy tends to respond to the impact of police incidents with more intensity than an experienced officer, he is, in general, protected from too demanding assignments, and shielded from danger. He may chafe under this restraint because he is eager to be tested. The day comes when he can hardly wait to enter the exciting life of the precinct.

The Academy training period lasts from four to six months. Graduation is a thrilling *rite de passage*. It means new uniforms, new group attachments, new responsibilities, oaths of allegiance, and a rise in status. The occasion is invested with solemnity and significance. For the majority of rookies without extensive educational backgrounds, it is a worthy substitute for college graduation.

The very next morning the graduate is rudely dumped into a strange precinct where he must prove himself.

CHAPTER 3

On the Job

The Rookie at the Precinct

The recruit reports to his precinct with some anxiety, but in general ready to practice what has been preached to him at the Academy. According to the general code of deportment, which covers the behavior of the newcomer, he is expected to be a good listener, quiet, unassuming, and deferential without being obsequious toward his superior officers. Despite a good deal of hazing as part of the breaking-in period the recruit usually adapts to these standards without difficulty.

For a month or so, he receives lenience and sympathy for routine mistakes. After that he is on trial and carefully watched to see how he measures up to the challenge of police patrol. His reputation is made in the next few weeks and will shadow him for the rest of his police career: no matter where or when he is transferred, a phone call will precede his arrival, reporting the evaluation that was made of his handling of his first few important cases.

On these cases the new patrolman must resolve the dilemma of choosing between the professional ideal of police work he has learned at the Academy and the pragmatic precinct approach. In the Academy, where professionalism is accented, the orientation is toward that of the social sciences and opposed to the "lock-them-up" philosophy. But in the precinct a patrolman is measured by his arrest record. Thus the new man is needled when he shows signs of diffidence in arresting or asserting his authority. Over and over again well-meaning old-timers reiterate, "You gotta be tough, kid, or you'll never last." Fifteen years ago Westley observed this phenomenon in the police force he studied and explained the basic rationalization behind the slogan:

> Expecting the excuse, the argument, the evasion, the officer tries to get tough first, to treat them tough, to make them respect the law, a particular judgment of the law. . . . This is the origin of the get tough, make them respect you thesis which predominates throughout police work.[1]

It is disconcerting to find that a similar solution to the practitioner-client problem is widely accepted in other service professions, that have none of the authoritarian flavor of the police force. In probation and parole work Lloyd Ohlin found that

> The (social) worker experiences widespread pressure by the police and other official functionaries to define his role as that of the enforcement officer who should use control measures to restrict the client's freedom and coercion to punish him for wrongdoing. When he attempts to resist these pressures, he finds probation and parole interpreted as leniency and himself identified as a "sob sister."[2]

According to Howard S. Becker's analysis of the teacher-pupil relationship, some teachers adopt the same attitude toward their charges:

> You can't ever let them get the upper hand on you or you're through. So I start out tough. . . . You've got to

[1] William A. Westley, "The Police: A Sociological Study of Law, Custom, and Morality," *op. cit.*, p. 112.
[2] Ohlin, *op. cit.*, p. 221.

start out tough then you can ease up as you go along. If you start out easy-going, when you try to get tough, they'll just look at you and laugh.[3]

That a "get tough" ideology dominates many workers in the major institutions devoted to the education, control, and welfare of the public is of prime importance to sociologists. Why should the field practitioner, in actual contact with the clientele he is supposed to serve, develop a philosophy so contrary to the creed of altruism and service that his profession exalts? Apparently, practical experience leads to the acceptance of a Hobbesian model of the social system.

In the case of the young policeman the choice between professionalism and pragmatism is apt to depend largely on the circumstances of the case. It is, for example, no great feat for a policeman working in an upper-class neighborhood to protect the rights of his white clientele. It is much more difficult in a lower-class community. In a slum area the professional ethic loses most of the time: the civil rights of lower-class individuals do not count as much as the necessity to accomplish a staggering amount of police work as expeditiously as possible. Shifting from idealism to pragmatism, the newcomer to a lower-class precinct house enters a new reference group whose members are a little contemptuous of all the Academy represents.

Learning the Ropes: Language

The identification with this new group is revealed in many facets of behavior and personality. Speech patterns increasingly reflect the loss of influence of Academy training, which

[3] Howard S. Becker, "Social Class Variations in the Teacher-Pupil Relationship," *Journal of Educational Sociology*, Vol. 25 (1951–1952), p. 459.

demanded a decent level of grammar and vocabulary. Police terminology, which substitutes broad stereotypes for precise distinctions, becomes a linguistic crutch. The colloquialism "desperate" means anything bad, unpleasant, or derogatory. "Radical" is used to label anyone who is not reactionary, or at least conservative, even those policemen who are articulate in protesting about long-accepted conditions in the department. A "detail" is a special job or assignment—usually a desirable one. "Rabbi" means a person with influence in the department. Although Jewish policemen suspect the dark origins of this neologism, they cannot help being amused when they overhear conversations like the following:

"Say, did you hear that O'Grady finally got that detail to the Detective Division?"

"No. But I knew that he had a contract in. Who was his rabbi?"

"His rabbi? Why his uncle, the priest, of course." The word "contract" is very important in the police world. It can mean any obligation, debt, errand, request, agreement, or arrangement.[4]

A whole class of colorful idioms is derived from parts of the body. "Hairy" stands for smart, shrewd, and conniving. "On the arm," and "egghead" are fairly well known in common parlance. A courageous policeman who stands up for his rights is complimented with the description, "he has a lot of balls."[5]

[4] There are varying degrees of obligation in each contract. When it is performed, a reciprocal obligation arises to fulfill a contract in return. Sometimes, in the performance of a contract, several intermediaries are approached in order to attain the final result. Each of these middlemen becomes enmeshed in this contractual web. Thus, it forms an unofficial system of rights and obligations that often controls interpersonal relations more stringently than do bureaucratic protocol and hierarchy.

[5] For a parallel study of the use of "body" terms in the jargon of an all-male society, see Henry Elkin, "Aggressive and Erotic Tendencies in Army Life," *American Journal of Sociology*, Vol. 51 (1945-1946), pp. 411-412.

In the precinct even the well-educated officers adopt this slovenly jargon, sometimes consciously, to merge their identities with those of the "common men" on the force. They purposely say mischiev-*i*-ous and mispronounce other common words in order to belong and conform.[6] The police role and its special argot cannot, however, be donned for eight hours a day without making serious inroads: when the time comes for the intellectual to slough off his occupational speech patterns, he is often unsuccessful, to his great embarrassment.

Although official police policy strongly condemns any reciprocity between policemen and criminal elements, it nonetheless exists and is mirrored in a shared vocabulary. This social interaction is unwittingly recognized as unavoidable by the authoritative *FBI Law Enforcement Bulletin*. The editors, listing a glossary of several hundred words and phrases commonly used by the underworld, are forced to justify the fact that at least one-half of the list is included in the police lexicon:

> Just as the newspaperman, the short-order cook, or the baseball player has a specialized manner of expressing himself, so has the juvenile gang member, the criminal and, by necessity, the police officer. . . .
>
> The words on pages 24, 25 are included in the jargon of the violator as well as that of the law enforcement officer, since it is difficult to separate one from the other. The policeman, finding it necessary to be cognizant of the criminal's lingo, frequently absorbs it as part of his own speech and uses the terms and phrases in his general police activities, as well as contributing to it many colorful forms of expression of his own.[7]

[6] In "The Intellectuals and the Language of Minorities," *American Journal of Sociology*, Vol. 64 (1958–1959), pp. 25–35, Melvin Seeman has shown that where intellectuals are minorities, they often employ defensive tactics of this type.

[7] "Juvenile Gangs and Underworld Have Own Lingo," *FBI Law Enforcement Bulletin*, Vol. 30 (January 1961), pp. 22–23.

Ritual

Along with a new vocabulary, the new patrolman also picks up a series of rituals, several of them vital to the world of the policeman. One—the "coffee and" ritual which began each tour of duty—operated with unforgettable potency during the time I was on the beat. Each day en route to his post the patrolman stopped almost compulsively at his favorite luncheonette or cafeteria for coffee and cake. Even when a tough "shoofly"[8] was reported in the vicinity, a "real" cop felt obliged to risk the chance of receiving a complaint to stop for his coffee. Since the ritual was followed even on sweltering summer days, it could not be related to his desire to warm up. It had nothing to do with hunger because in most cases the men came to work just after a heavy meal. It was not a "break" to relieve fatigue; the tour was just starting. In some manner the coffee seemed to allay the vestige of anxiety every thinking policeman carries with him on his tour of patrol. Life and death are so closely bound up with police work that the ceremonious interruption, like a religious duty, may have constituted a libation to the gods.

Foot Patrol

The basic job of the police force is patrol, where most recruits start. The patrolman pounding his beat is the proletarian of the department, and, like proletarians in most coun-

---

[8] A "shoofly" is a supervisor of patrol who purposely dresses in civilian clothes rather than in proper uniform in order to avoid being spotted by the men on patrol.

tries, accorded a very low status. His position has been real-
istically described in the *Police Management Review*, issued
by the Planning Bureau of the New York City Police Department:

> Yet, more than anyone else in the Department, the foot
> patrolman is prone to boredom and inertia. Young and ini-
> tially enthusiastic men are often bored at a time when a
> proportion of the Force is overworked.[9]

> The working hours of the foot patrolman, the recurrent
> bad publicity, the indifferent attitudes of the public, the
> fact that promotion and earnings are almost completely
> divorced from the performance of his duties, all constitute
> an imposing array of anti-motivating factors.[10]

The patrolman can find little satisfaction in his work when
something goes wrong on his post; although the investigation
starts at the very top, inevitably the "buck" is passed down
until the final responsibility and blame come to rest upon him.
When, however, praise is lavished, some superior officer or
member of the force in a special assignment appears from
nowhere to accept the accolade. Moreover, the patrolman,
although he does a little of everything, is being increasingly
restricted to trivialities because police work is constantly de-
veloping specialties that only trained experts can handle. Just
when the work becomes most interesting, a specialist is assigned to replace the lowly "man on the post."

In the exciting cases, such as homicides or serious felonies,
the patrolman on post must notify the station house as soon
as he discovers the incident. Within minutes, a superior officer
from the Detective Division assumes command. From then
on the patrolman is a supernumerary. Detectives swarm over
the scene searching for clues, interviewing witnesses and sus-

---

[9] Lieutenant Matthew J. Neary, "Motivating the Foot Patrolman," *Police
Management Review* (November 1963), p. 5.
[10] *Ibid.*, p. 7.

pects, handling specific parts of the investigation. The Photo Unit arrives to take pictures. The Mobile Laboratory rolls up and scientific instruments are trundled into the crime area. The patrolman, shunted to one side, is sometimes allowed to guard the scene, by which time he may be wondering just how necessary he really is. It may, however, be worth noting that even the detective who supplants the patrolman will have only a moment of glory if he solves the case. The computer has invaded the world of the police. Soon the only record of his achievement will be a few holes punched on an I.B.M. card stockpiled in some basement storeroom. Alienation may not be as universal a condition in contemporary society as some social critics allege, but a computerized milieu fosters foreboding uneasiness.

The foot patrolman with heavy responsibility but no prestige either on or off the job becomes first bitter, then apathetic. Many times I have asked a young patrolman how many years he has had on the job. A common response is, "I have seventeen years, four months, two weeks, and three days to go until retirement." Small wonder that the score of foot patrolmen on the cynicism questionnaire was significantly higher than the mean score of the total sample.

Keeping the Law

Another potent source of cynicism is the new policeman's realization that it is literally impossible to enforce every law "on the book"—the jails would be too small to hold the prisoners—and that one of the important arts he must master is the sense of when to take action and, perhaps more important, when not to. An officer who brings too many trivial cases into the station house is considered incompetent, but an officer who brings in too few is considered a shirker.

The conventional wisdom of the job sets the standard. The old sages of the station house dispense didactic tales to which new members of the force listen avidly, thereby learning that typical incidents to be settled on the street, or occasionally even dodged, are the annoying drunk, the case of disorderly conduct involving adolescents who congregate on street corners, and quarrels between: husband and wife, taxi driver and his fare, neighbor and neighbor, store owner and customer, and landlord and tenants.

When an officer clearly observes a serious violation of law, his discretion is limited; he must arrest. But the average crime is not committed in full view of the policeman. He must conduct a preliminary investigation which places him in the middle of a labyrinth, following conflicting reports of witnesses into blind alleys. Each suspect denies any connection with the crime. Perpetrators claim to be victims. From time to time progress is barred by a wall of silence. Shall he make an arrest or not? Which of the suspects should he arrest? Just when he needs them most, the usual guideposts are silent. His wisest procedure is to trust no one. Cynicism improves his technique as an investigator.[11]

It is the individual policeman's responsibility to decide if and how the law should be applied, and he searches for the proper combination of cues on which to base his decision. These are derived from the typical sociological variables: class, education, clarity of role prescriptions, reference groups, self-conception, and visibility. Because the application of the law depends to a large degree on the definition of

---

[11] Despite his typical mistrust, the average policeman fancies himself a keen psychologist, who can by intuition, and/or experience, sense when a person being interrogated is lying or telling the truth.

the situation and the decision reached by the patrolman, he, in effect, makes the law; it is his decision that establishes the boundary between legal and illegal.

Always searching for this tenuous and blurred dividing line in the behavior of others, the policeman frequently loses the ability to distinguish between law and license in himself. As the result of United States Supreme Court decisions, kaleidoscopic changes in the practical application of the law have confused the average patrolman until he is often uncertain of the proper course of action. His ignorance dims the luster of the law because the policeman learns to manipulate law in the name of expediency, and this loss of respect, in turn, breeds more cynicism.

In the administration of justice, the poor, the minorities, and the deviants need all the protection possible. They suffer most when the police fail to take proper action. In busy precincts covering sections inhabited by Negroes or Puerto Ricans, this sphere of inaction is large. Incidents that would cause commotion and consternation in quiet precincts seem so common in ghetto neighborhoods that they are often not reported. The police rationalize this avoidance of duty with theories that the victim would refuse to prosecute because violence has become the accepted way of life for his community, and that any other course would result in a great loss of time in court, which would reduce the efficiency of other police functions. These decisions are rarely subjected to review, a particularly disturbing situation to men who are interested in creating a better system of justice.[12]

[12] Joseph Goldstein, "Police Discretion Not to Invoke the Criminal Process: Low Visibility Decisions in the Administration of Justice," *The Yale Law Journal*, Vol. 69 (1960), pp. 574–575. See also Herman Goldstein, "Police Discretion: The Ideal Versus the Real," *Public Administration Review*, Vol. 23 (September 1963), pp. 140–148; and Wayne R. LaFave, *Arrest: The Decision to Take a Suspect into Custody* (Boston: Little, Brown and Co., 1965).

Police decisions not to invoke the criminal process largely determine the outer limits of law enforcement. By such decisions, the police define the ambit of discretion through-out the process of other decision-makers—prosecutor, grand and petit jury, judge, probation officer, correction authority, and parole and pardon boards. These police decisions, unlike their decisions to invoke the law, are of extremely low visibility and consequently are seldom the subject of review. Yet an opportunity for review and appraisal of non-enforcement decisions is essential to the functioning of the rule of law in our system of criminal justice.[13]

When the professionals attack this non-enforcement of the law, the articulate defender of the status quo has a powerful riposte: he can plead that the social sciences so profusely quoted by the professionals also teach the lesson of cultural relativity. This doctrine encourages an observer from one culture to respect the integrity of another, although its standards of behavior may be different from his own. The implication is that the policeman has some justification for accepting a minority group's way of life on its own terms, and thus for acting the way he does. There is no easy answer to this paradox.

A harsher indictment of the police officer's neglect or refusal to enforce the law has been pronounced by Martin Luther King who holds that nonfeasance amounts to malfeasance:

The most grievous charge against municipal police is not brutality, although it exists. Permissive crime in ghettos is the nightmare of the slum family. Permissive crime is the name for the organized crime that flourishes in the ghetto—designed, directed, and cultivated by white national crime syndicates operating numbers, narcotics, and prostitution

[13] Joseph Goldstein, *op. cit.*, p. 543.

rackets freely in the protected sanctuaries of the ghettos. Because no one, including the police, cares particularly about ghetto crime, it pervades every area of life.[14]

The Summons

Even the routine, apparently trivial duties that the young policeman must learn to handle may easily escalate into a near riot unless he controls them properly. Take, for example, the serving of a summons on a peddler. The public observing this event is apt to react with hostility toward the policeman. The officer himself may feel a little guilty.

This appears to be a universal dilemma for policemen. Anatole France has written a short story, "Crainquebille,"[15] which depicts the repercussions in the life of a French vegetable seller when Constable 64 arrests him for peddling. When the policeman orders Crainquebille to move on, the vendor mutters something under his breath which sounds to the policeman like "*Mort aux Vaches,*" in those days, a vile insult that meant literally "Death to the Cows," but was interpreted as "Down with the Cops."[16]

During World War II, a New York City policeman had an equally harrowing experience with a peddler, selling pretzels, who set up her daily shop in front of a well-known department store. One of the patrolman's important duties was to keep the post clear of peddlers, by no means an easy assignment on a busy shopping day. Although Molly, as we shall call her, was small and elderly, she had the strength and speed

[14] Martin Luther King, "Beyond the Los Angeles Riots: Next Stop: The North," *Saturday Review,* Vol. 48 (November 13, 1965), p. 34.
[15] Anatole France, "Crainquebille," in *Golden Tales of Anatole France* (New York: Dodd Mead and Co., 1926), pp. 215–257.
[16] It is interesting to note that in France the police were called "cows" in the vernacular, but to Americans the police are "bulls."

of an athlete. She dexterously threaded her way through the crowds, unseen by the police until she set down her basket at a suitable spot. No matter how many times she was chased away, she always reappeared.

One day the patrolman became so exasperated that he decided to serve her with a summons. At the sight of his summons book, Molly began to scream, "Murderer! He's killing me! Why doesn't he catch criminals instead of ruining a poor woman who is trying to make an honest living? Nazi!" With this she threw herself down on the ground, and rolled around in a fit of fury or despair, never stopping the stream of epithets. The policeman (who was Jewish himself) was thoroughly embarrassed by the obvious rancor of the crowd of hundreds gathered to watch the show. Arrest seemed the only answer, and in desperation he asked a bystander to call the precinct for a patrol wagon.

After a struggle, he placed Molly and her heavy pretzel basket into the wagon, climbed in himself, and signaled the driver to proceed. Suddenly he noticed a transformation in the prisoner. The histrionics had stopped. As they slowly pulled away from the scene, Molly peered intently through the rear grating, a quiet smile of triumph on her face. The officer glanced out. From the subway kiosk Molly's husband, Abie, was emerging, loaded down with an overflowing basket of pretzels, certain of a couple of uninterrupted hours of brisk sales. It was impossible to escape the suspicion of prearrangement.

Police management hotly denies the existence of a summons quota. Men at the patrol level are not so sure about this. In November 1960 there was a well-publicized altercation between then New York Police Commissioner Kennedy and Patrolman John J. Cassese, the president of the Patrolmen's

Benevolent Association. Patrolman Cassese bought advertising space in the New York City press in which he alleged that there was definitely a quota system, and that he could prove it.[17] Thereupon the delegates to the P.B.A. were given questionnaires demanding whether or not they knew of any summons quota system. According to the *Herald Tribune*, delegates who answered negatively admitted later that they had lied[18] to keep from having to reveal the names of the superior officers responsible for ordering the quota system. The so-called "rat rule" requires a member of the force having knowledge of a violation of departmental regulations to report it to a superior officer, but these policemen preferred to perjure themselves rather than be known as informers.[19]

Graft

Every policeman patrolling the streets sooner or later faces the temptation of a "payoff." As in most other large organizations, there are the few who have their price, but their betrayal of the public trust has unjustifiably tarnished the whole department. The image of the crooked cop projected in literature has fortified this misconception. In *The Iceman Cometh*, Eugene O'Neill described ex-Lieutenant Pat Mc-

[17] It is of interest that Commissioner Kennedy on December 9, 1959, sent a teletype message to all commands explaining why there could not be a quota: "Inasmuch as there is no quota on persons killed and injured, there cannot be and there is no quota on enforcement." See New York *Herald Tribune*, November 29, 1960, p. 15.

[18] New York *Herald Tribune*, November 29, 1960, pp. 1, 15.

[19] A statement concerning the existence of a summons quota was included in the cynicism questionnaire. Well over half the patrolmen, and more than forty per cent of the superior officers apparently do believe that a summons quota exists (see Appendix).

Gloin as "the biggest drunken grafter that ever disgraced the police force." McGloin's former position lures him, and his one hope is to be reinstated because "there's fine pickings these days."[20] Actual policemen seem to accept graft for other reasons than avarice. Often the first transgression is inadvertent. Or, they may be gradually indoctrinated by older policemen. Step by step they progress from a small peccadillo to outright shakedown and felony.

A Denver policeman involved in the police burglary scandal of 1961 recalls his downfall.

> So the rookie . . . is turned over to a more experienced man for breaking in. . . .
>
> He knows he is being watched. . . . He is eager to be accepted.
>
> He does what he can to show he has guts. He backs up his partner in any way he can. . . .
>
> It may happen like this: the older man stops at a bar, comes out with some packages of cigarettes. He does this several times. He explains that this is part of the job. . . .
>
> So he, the rookie, goes into a Skid Row bar and stands uncomfortably at the end, waiting for the bartender to acknowledge his presence and disdainfully toss him two packages of butts.
>
> The feeling of pride slips away, and a hint of shame takes hold.
>
> One thing leads to another for the rookies. After six months they have become conditioned to accept free meals, a few packs of cigarettes, turkeys at Thanksgiving and liquor at Christmas from the respectable people in their districts. . . .[21]

Lincoln Steffens, one of the great muckrakers, studied police corruption in New York and other cities at the end of

[20] Eugene O'Neill, *The Iceman Cometh* (New York: Random House, 1946), pp. 55, 57.
[21] Mort Stern, "What Makes a Policeman Go Wrong?" *Journal of Criminal Law, Criminology and Police Science*, Vol. 53 (March 1962), pp. 98–99.

the nineteenth century.[22] His report of the Schmittberger saga is documented by the records of the Lexow Commission. The blemished hero of the story is a baker named Schmittberger who became a member of the New York City Police Department and was assigned to the Tenderloin district. He was so honest, and so dumb, that when someone came up to him one day and put ten dollars in his hand while he was on patrol, he immediately turned it over to his captain. The captain was so impressed by this honesty, that he rewarded Schmittberger in the most fitting way possible—by making him his graft collection man. Schmittberger showed great talent for his new job. Finally he turned State's evidence during the Lexow investigation and thus retained his job. Theodore Roosevelt, the new Police Commissioner, was eager to eliminate vice in the city and corruption in the department. Steffens advised him to rely upon Schmittberger as the spearhead of the campaign. Schmittberger, the most assiduous collector of graft under the former regime, responded by devoting his tremendous energy and experience to the problem of arresting or outlawing gamblers and prostitutes.

Schmittberger's initial encounter with graft was not unique. The pattern has repeated itself through the years. A similar case from the 1940's, involved a young policeman who held a college degree. The commanding officer of the precinct, favorably impressed by the patrolman's obvious attempt to do a good job, called him into his office to discuss the problem of organized gambling in the precinct and shortly after assigned him to a special park post to arrest, if possible,

[22] Lincoln Steffens, *The Shame of the Cities* (New York: McClure Phillips & Co., 1904); Lincoln Steffens, *The Autobiography of Lincoln Steffens* (New York: Harcourt, Brace & Co., 1931). For one of the latest of the many books on the subject of police corruption, see Ralph L. Smith, *The Tarnished Badge* (New York: Thomas Y. Crowell Co., 1965).

the suspected bookmakers who were supposed to operate in the area.

The park was as famous as Hyde Park in London. Radicals and political dissenters of every persuasion made it their headquarters. On the crosswalks, rival speakers harangued listeners and thundered against each other, the system, and the "lackeys of the ruling class." Our college-trained patrolman grew so familiar with the appellation that he did not even flinch at it, but thought it odd that they were berating him for protecting their right to fulminate against the power elite. He was in his element. College had prepared him for such an assignment.

Among the various groups—some arguing vociferously, others deeply immersed in the latest *Daily Worker*—the officer walked his post with a smug sense of accomplishment. What other officer could mediate so well among Stalinists, Trotskyites, Lovestone-ites, Nazis, and Fascists? Whether it was dialectic materialism, united front, permanent revolution, or any of the other current political clichés, our hero could handle himself well.

He became a species of referee to whom disputants would appeal for redress. A supporter of the Fascists would accost him and whisper to him that a dangerous "Red" with a knife had threatened to stab him. A Trotskyite might slip him a note containing allegations against a Nazi. He did a wonderful job of controlling the political tempers and wars in the park. But he never noticed any sign of bookmaking or gambling.

This went on for several months. One winter night about 6:00 P.M. almost everyone had deserted the park because it was raining heavily. One persistent group, however, was still busily engaged in a discussion of some abstruse point in the

Worker. The patrolman approached them and, wanting to get them out of the park so he could "grab a fast cup of coffee," called out roughly, "Why don't you go home? Here you are trying to settle the world's problems and you don't even know enough to get out of the rain." The apparent leader of the group said, "Officer, I'll speak to you later." The officer, anticipating the usual accusations against rival groups in the park, responded, "Don't bother speaking to me at all. Just pack up and get out of here." Then he turned and walked away.

He heard someone follow him from the group and felt a wad of paper thrust stealthily into his hand. Certain that it was another "piece of vital information" he looked at it contemptuously. He was shocked to see that this time there were two bills in his palm.

When he saw his side partner, Big Fred, he eagerly told the story. Big Fred looked at him queerly and said, "That was Izzy, the bookie. Do you mean to tell me you've been working in the park this whole time and don't know Izzy?" At that moment the rookie saw how far he had to travel before he became a real "cop." The bookie and his horseplayers had been busy all those weeks discussing, not the Third International at Moscow but the Third Invitational at Hialeah. Behind every *Daily Worker* had been a copy of the *Daily Racing Form.*

The strange thing is that a policeman can take the payoff and still consider himself an honest or innocent man. The Denver policeman reacted to graft by saying:

> that this is okay, that all the men accept these things, that this is a far cry from stealing and they can still be good policemen.[23]

[23] Mort Stern, *op. cit.,* p. 99.

Lincoln Steffens gives a more involved explanation to the same effect.

> The collections, he, Schmittberger, was to make for his captain were the regular monthly payments by gamblers, prostitutes, saloons—all law-breakers—for the privilege of breaking the law, rightly called police protection. . . .
>
> The big business was the regular graft that Schmittberger handled for years, all in the day's work, without losing either his honesty or, it seemed to me, all his innocence. I often afterward reviewed this part of his experience; it bore upon my old interest in moral and ethical psychology. My note was that the process of corruption had begun so quietly with the first tip and proceeded so gradually in an environment where it was all a matter of course, that this man never realized what he was doing till the Lexow Committee's exposure.[24]

Knowing that the Penal Law and the police regulations clearly prohibit such malfeasance, how is it possible for an experienced policeman to accept money, and at the same time maintain that he is innocent of any wrongdoing? Such psychological prestidigitation can be accomplished only by artful casuistry based on cynicism. The policeman rationalizes with twisted logic: "I am not hurting anyone. Everyone is doing the same thing. Most people are much worse. The public thinks a policeman is dishonest whether he is or not. Therefore, I am not doing anything wrong by taking graft."

The Arrest

The function of the police department that justifies the claim of professional status is crime prevention. This special

[24] Lincoln Steffens, *The Autobiography of Lincoln Steffens, op. cit.,* pp. 272–273.

function is measured, validly or not, by the "good pinch." Not only the public, but also the police themselves accept this standard; as a result, they glorify the felony arrest.

> The apprehension of the felon then represents for these men a source of prestige in the police department . . . and in the community.[25]

Yet according to the research division of the International Association of Chiefs of Police, "the percentage of the police effort devoted to the traditional criminal law matters probably does not exceed ten per cent."[26] Police forces have been overwhelmed with onerous administrative and regulative duties which keep them from devoting their major attention to preventing crime. Moreover, the advocates of professionalism, by stressing the qualities of police integrity rather than mere performance, have given a curious twist to the act of arrest. It is well known that gambling syndicates are the commonest source of police corruption. Thus the professionals on the force hail the arrest of a known gambler or bookie as a great feat and often allow it to assume more significance than an arrest for a serious felony. The patrolman, not sharing the professionals' artificial viewpoint on this subject, never considers the bookie as a criminal in the same class with a rapist or a mugger, and explains the peculiar reversal of values in which a "bookie's" arrest is a cause for more

[25] Westley, "The Police: A Sociological Study of Law, Custom, and Morality," *op. cit.*, p. 225.

[26] Richard A. Myren and Lynn D. Swanson, *Police Contacts with Juveniles: Perspectives, Guidelines, 2nd Review Draft,* June 1961 (Washington, D.C.: Children's Bureau, United States Department of Health, Education, and Welfare, 1961), pp. 1–4. In an empirical study of the Syracuse Police Department, 801 incoming telephone calls were analyzed over a period of eighty-two hours in the summer of 1961. Only twenty per cent of the calls were related to crime or violence. See Elaine Cumming, Ian M. Cumming, and Laura Edell, "Policeman as Philosopher, Guide and Friend," *Social Problems*, Vol. 12 (Winter 1965), p. 279.

celebration than a felony arrest is by ascribing either stupidity or hypocrisy to the "big brass."

One overpowering reason for cynicism among patrolmen is that it stimulates an outstanding arrest record. The very cynical officer rejects the possibility of decent impulses in others. By undertaking many investigations and never letting up in his relentless justification of this morbid distrust, he is following the advice laid down by the experts. For example, in the obituary of James Leggett, former Chief of Detectives of the New York City Police Department, the New York *Times* reported that Leggett frequently urged his subordinates to probe, probe, probe, until they came up with the answers.

> You have to be nosey, use your eyes and your ears, and continually ask questions. . . .
> Keep saying to yourself, over and over, "What's the answer?" Take nothing for granted. . . .[27]

A high arrest record reinforces the cynicism that inspired it in the first place, while often establishing a policeman's reputation for initiative and efficiency. His superiors recommend him for assignment to the detective division. This route to promotion appeals to many young policemen who have little hope of passing a written competitive test for promotion, and impels many of them to adopt cynicism as a rational and functional way to advancement.

The Five Year Man

By the time a patrolman has had five years on the force, he has usually started casting about for a "good detail" in

[27] New York *Times*, January 17, 1962, p. 33.

order to escape from foot patrol duty. Upon hearing rumors
of impending transfers, patrolmen seek to arrange "contracts
with rabbis." The lower ranks tend to believe that special
assignments depend on "whom you know," and not on
merit.[28]

In most cases, detective work is the detail preferred above
all others. However, most policemen will accept any detail
"as long as I get 'out of the bag' (uniform)." Defining this
as simply the desire for upward mobility would be short-
sighted. The implications go much deeper to reveal the policemen's urge to escape from foot patrol duty in uniform,
not only because of its low status, but also because a large
proportion of the men become "fed up" with this basic job
of all police systems. Their service motivation has become
extinguished: they want to remove the uniform that publicly
identifies them as policemen.

This desire impels many officers to prepare for the second
ladder of upward mobility, the civil service promotion test.
Day after day the patrolman studying for the sergeant's examination plods his way to the "cram" school, sometimes to
two or three schools on consecutive days. There are men
who have been attending such classes for twenty years,
and are still optimistic.

All too quickly, the policeman moves along his career line.
Until his twelfth year there is the possibility of leaving police
work for a more attractive and remunerative position. After
this, he realizes that in only eight more years he will be entitled to a pension, and his desire to leave quickly diminishes.

[28] In the study of cynicism forty per cent of the patrolmen shared this
view (Appendix item 13), in the face of strong protestations to the contrary by top officials of the department.

The Jewish Patrolman

The Great Depression was mainly responsible for the entry of a number of Jews into the classically Irish police force.[29] In those days Jews faced prejudice. The prevailing attitudes toward them were of thinly disguised contempt, and disbelief that they would make good cops. Jewish policemen were forced to prove themselves worthy.

One Jewish patrolman finally convinced the opposition. He won so many awards for his police work that his nickname became "Medals." But his finest hour came when the other policemen, and his personal friends outside the force, started calling him "Reilly." There were not many Jewish "Reillys" at the beginning.

Jewish policemen faced more than prejudice. A high percentage of these newcomers were college men. They naturally became the target for the anti-intellectualism that policemen shared with many other Americans. A Jewish policeman with a college degree soon realized that for him the police world was out of joint. His handling of police situations often seemed feasible by college standards, but frequently was impractical according to the standards of traditional police practice. With middle-class antecedents, and his Jewish heritage, he almost inevitably attempted to solve problems verbally rather than by force.

There are several recurrent, unpleasant situations that confront the Jewish policeman. Often the non-Jewish policeman

[29] Nathan Glazer and Daniel P. Moynihan, *Beyond the Melting Pot* (Cambridge: The M.I.T. Press and Harvard University Press, 1964), p. 261.

tries to be friendly by hailing him with *"Mach a leben?"*
To the non-Jew this remark is equivalent to saying, "How
are things?" To the Jew it not only is bad grammar, but also
covertly insinuates that Jews are mainly interested in making
money. It is also difficult for the Jewish policeman to deal
with an anti-Semitic civilian. The problem is complicated by
the fact that anti-Semites are reputedly sensitive to Jewishness and able to recognize a Jew quickly but are fooled by
the police uniform which they associate with the Irish, or at
least non-Jewish policemen. Repeatedly an anti-Semite will
sidle up to the Jewish policeman and "out of a clear sky"
start blaming the evils of the world on the Jews. Only a
little less irritating to his pride as a policeman is the reaction
of the Jewish occupants of a car that he has stopped for a
traffic violation. The officer will hear them say in Yiddish,
"Give him a few dollars to forget the ticket, and let's get out
of here."

Today relative deprivation describes the state of Jewish
patrolmen. A generation ago Jewish policemen, compared
with members of different faiths or ethnic groups, had real
grievances, they were discriminated against and treated as
inferiors. Deprivation was not at all relative but absolute. Except in isolated instances this is no longer true. If the Jewish
policeman experiences frustration today, it is probably due to
his commitment to the traditional Jewish *Weltanschauung*
from which he is not completely emancipated. This tradition
is typified by the advice their leaders gave Jewish immigrants
near the end of the nineteenth century:

> Select a goal and pursue it with all your might. No matter
> what happens to you, hold on. You will experience a bad
> time but sooner or later you will achieve your goal. . . . A
> bit of advice for you: Do not take a moment's rest. Run,

do, work, and keep your own good in mind. . . . A final
virtue is needed in America—called cheek. . . . Do not say,
I cannot; I do not know.[30]

Jewish mothers-in-law have learned subtle techniques to
disguise their disappointment at having gained a policeman
son-in-law when they lost their daughter in marriage. For
example, one mother-in-law bravely surmounted her loss of
status by introducing her policeman son-in-law as a college
graduate with two degrees. Others try to conceal the police
blemish by describing the policeman relative as "in youth
work" or, if he is lucky enough to be attached to the Police
Academy, as "a teacher."

Jewish parents look forward to the wonderful day when
they can proudly introduce their offspring with the ritual
words, "My son, the doctor." It cannot give them the same
degree of satisfaction to present, "My son, the cop." They
suspect their friends of translating the words "My son, the
cop" into an altogether different phrase "My cop-son." It is
one of those ironical coincidences that in the Yiddish colloquial
speech the term of mild contempt commonly used to signify
"a person who will never amount to anything" is pronounced
phonetically "*cop son*."

While contemporary Jews have no high regard for police
work as an occupation, older Jewish people remember the
old-country ghettos, and the respect they were forced to
display to policemen. On the other hand, since several European nations barred Jews from the police force, émigré Jews
are often secretly proud that in America a Jew can become an
influential official with the power of life and death over

[30] Moses Rischin, *The Promised City: New York's Jews 1870–1914* (Cambridge: Harvard University Press, 1962), p. 75.

others. This ambivalence is mirrored in the attitude of Jewish policemen who sometimes feel like failures, but are often inwardly proud that they have succeeded in an occupation that once had this particular significance for their forebears.

The Detective

Crime novels often portray police department detectives as stupid, sadistic, lecherous, and altogether second-rate when compared with the "private eye"—that omniscient and ithyphallic standard-bearer of all that is noble. Erle Stanley Gardner, who mass-produces "whodunits" and qualifies as an expert on this phase of American culture, has some interesting and relevant opinions:

> And as far as detective fiction is concerned, the "dumb" cop is a fixture because the public demands him! In fact, it is as necessary to have a "dumb" cop in a detective story as it is to have a clever detective.
>
> For some years now, I have been interested in better law enforcement and my conscience got to bothering me about the manner in which Perry Mason pulled an intellectual razzle-dazzle on the dumb cops I had created in my books. Therefore, I decided to write a book in which I would show the police in their true colors and in which Mason would race neck and neck to a solution with the character who had previously taken the part of the dumb cop. The result was that the publisher was literally deluged with letters of protest from book dealers and public alike.[31]

Contrary to the fantasies of the paperback thrillers, the public actually accords great respect and prestige to the de-

[31] Erle Stanley Gardner, "The Need for New Concepts in the Administration of Criminal Justice," *Journal of Criminal Law, Criminology and Police Science*, Vol. 50 (May–June 1959), p. 22.

tective, far more than it grants to the uniformed beat patrolman. A detective's clothes, mannerisms, easy familiarity with superior officers, and snobbish aloofness from uniformed patrolmen are all part of his impressive front, helping him to dramatize his status and work performance. Within the police hierarchy the detective also enjoys an exalted status. Almost every cop dreams of the day when he will "make the bureau" and become a "big dick." Commissioners grant assignment to the detective bureau as a reward for exceptional performance. All members of the force know the benefits of detective work. Most imagine many more than exist, but there are three immediately apparent advantages: higher salary, more interesting work, and "getting out of the bag."

> Nearly every patrolman who comes into the department dreams of one day "making the bureau." He glories in thoughts of working in street clothes, sometimes in the most deceptive disguises, tracking down a dangerous gunman, searching for a clue at the scene of a homicide, lifting a fingerprint from a bloodied axe handle. . . .[32]

Candidates for detective units are usually given some preparatory training at the Police Academy. Their anticipatory socialization immediately displays itself. Their clothes take on an "Ivy" look: jackets, hats, carefully knotted ties, and trench coats replace the sweaters, lumberjackets, and hunters' caps worn by the less fortunate patrolmen.

Detectives are the upper class of police society and haughtily guard their special status and privileges. Their quarters are separate from those of the uniformed force. Within this private domain democratic camaraderie eliminates the social distance that ordinarily divides the various ranks of a bureaucratic hierarchy. A lower-ranking detective may call a detective captain by his first name without causing any surprise;

[32] *Spring 3100*, Vol. 30 (July–August 1959), p. 15.

he may walk arm-in-arm with a detective inspector (a very high superior officer), while discussing an important case.

Some cynics explain this nonchalant disregard of organizational protocol as the result of nepotism in department appointments. They claim that since almost every detective must have an important "rabbi," to get in the division no clever operator would risk antagonizing some unknown and powerful sponsor by being rude to his protégé, and thus adopts a friendly and democratic policy toward subordinates.

Because of the higher status of detectives within the department, a new policeman tends to assume that they are superior to uniformed men in intelligence or motivation. A strong minority on the force asserts on the contrary that a detective's value and future success depend on the private sources of information at his disposal, and his willingness to do the necessary leg work. They support this opinion by citing the many brilliant detectives in police history who could never have passed an I.Q. test, could hardly write an intelligible report, and whose techniques of investigation constantly violated every recommended principle of scientific detection.

Unexpected corroboration for this minority belief comes from a fabled detective whose heyday was forty years ago. As head of New York City's famed Italian Squad, which successfully battled the Mafia, Lieutenant Fiaschetti spoke with authority about the requirements for success as a detective, and evaluated the storybook detective intellectual rather pungently:

> It makes me tired to read how those bulls in books solve mysteries with their deductions. In the honest-to-God story of how the detective gets his man, stool pigeon's the word.[33]

[33] Michael Fiaschetti, *You Gotta Be Rough* (New York: Doubleday Doran & Co., 1930), p. 27.

It is also true that ambitious detectives strive to build up a private circle of informers which automatically connects them to the criminal underworld.

This interaction between detective and criminal is by no means confined to the American police force. In London, Scotland Yard sometimes depends on streetwalkers for tips. The effectiveness of this liaison was demonstrated after prostitutes were forbidden to solicit on the streets. As one Scotland Yard detective complained,

> One quite eccentric result of the street clearing was shown almost immediately by a series of successful jewel robberies at night in London which caught the police unprepared. "It's the fault of that Act," said one of the detectives to the press. "The girls used to notice when anything funny was up—they hadn't much else to do walking about—and they'd tip us off." Nowadays, the police depend on the ordinary marks, and have to do without streetgirl volunteers. It wasn't a very wide or reliable source of information; but it was something.[34]

The freedom of the detective division to form and utilize contacts with the criminal world underlines the peculiarly open structure of this segment of the police force. With its easygoing approach to interpersonal relations, its lack of concern for the formal regulations that hamstring the rest of the department, and its informal discipline, the division forms what might be called a mock bureaucracy.[35] It is of special

[34] Raymond Postgate, "London: Goodbye to Hullo, Darling," *Holiday Magazine*, Vol. 28 (November 1960), p. 50.

[35] In *Patterns of Industrial Bureaucracy* (Glencoe: The Free Press, 1954), Alvin Gouldner describes three theoretical types of bureaucracy: the punishment-centered, the representative, and the mock. All three types can be found among police departments. The traditional police force with its authoritarian structure corresponds to the punishment-centered bureaucracy. The professional force stresses a persuasive, more democratic kind of discipline, and can be equated to the representative type. The detective division, of course, fits nicely into the description of the mock bureaucracy.

significance that this high-status unit, to which every member of the lower echelon aspires, performs best when disregarding formal regulations and official procedures. Adopting detectives as models, other members of the force do not remain as fervently dedicated to these official rules and procedures as they might if they lacked this example.

The Superior Officer

Superior officers of the old regime were autocrats. Patrolmen responded fearfully to their wrath and would not have risked approaching them casually. Supervisors were quick to register complaints, generally about subordinates who failed to acknowledge a superior's innate charisma.

In contemporary police culture, democratization and demilitarization have replaced the formerly rigid code, for several reasons. In the first place, there is no police counterpart of West Point at which the superior officer may be trained (although the National Academy of the Federal Bureau of Investigation gradually has attained an equivalence). In America police superiors rise from the ranks and have no aura of glamour, upper-class background, or unique endowments with which to impress the rank and file. A superior's reputation precedes him; he cannot expect to be treated with rigid deference.

The influx of college men into police work during and after the Great Depression upset the established pattern of upward mobility within the ranks. Educated policemen were able to shorten by half the time required for promotion to sergeant. After World War II, many men transferred from the armed forces to the police. Fed up with ostentatious rituals, combat veterans coined barbed epithets for those who insisted on exaggerated compliance with protocol, and consequently helped to democratize patterns of interaction in the police system. Professionalization also accelerated this process. Policemen, regarding themselves as experts and leaders, became involved in role conflicts. Trying to impress the public with his leadership, the policeman only perfunctorily salutes or otherwise recognizes differences in rank, and thus compromises his professional self-conception and the demands of protocol.

The current loosening of rigid discipline is so evident that police administrators are beginning to classify the sergeant as a foreman in industry who has allied himself with labor rather than with management. Some police experts, unwilling or unable to accept the sergeant's reduced prestige, consider it a damaging blow to the force and to the community. In the following comments, Paul Weston, a high-ranking police officer before he became a college professor of Police Administration, expresses the sentiments of the old regime.

> A slow eating or wearing away of the responsibility and authority of a patrol sergeant has been taking place. If it is not halted, this deterioration will undermine the entire hierarchy of any police unit, contribute to the waste of human resources, and interfere with attempts to gain objectives which will provide a community with a climate of law and order.[36]

While top level management and even friendly sergeants may be somewhat responsible for this transformation, Weston feels that the true miscreants are industrial sociologists and psychologists, who

> preach the creed that a happy worker is an efficient and productive worker. "Fear," they said, "should never rule."

[36] Paul Weston, "The Role of the Patrol Sergeant," *Law and Order*, Vol. 7 (September 1959), p. 31.

Requests and suggestions, instead of orders, would keep the workers happy.

These experts in human relations in industry say that supervision should not be brutal and reign through fear, and that supervisors must like people, help them, and constantly strive to get along with them. While it is true that brutality has no place in supervision, it is possible that fear can have its constructive aspects.

Every police department has one or more "tough" sergeants. Men who appear to dislike people, offer little apparent help, and seem to have little or no interest in getting along with them. This type of supervisor commands respect despite the environment of fear he creates, and though he sets high standards of performance, he is usually as demanding of himself as he is of his subordinates. Men may not like him, but they like working for him, and he develops subordinates as he spurs them to peak performance.[37]

---

[37] *Ibid.*, The reduction of the social distance between superiors and subordinates has not yet reduced the policeman's traditional distrust of the disciplinary system. There were three items in the cynicism study (see Appendix) that pertained to this topic. In item 1, only two of the sample of eighty-four patrolmen agreed that the average police superior is very interested in the welfare of his subordinates. More than one-half of the eighty-four thought that superiors were mostly concerned with their own problems.

In statement 2, three-quarters of the patrolman sample chose the C alternative to the effect that the average departmental complaint is the result of the pressure on superior officers from higher authority to give out complaints. It is notable that more than fifty per cent of the superior officers also accept this completion as the most nearly correct.

The answers to the third question on this point (item 9) indicated a general loss of faith in the disciplinary system. More than fifty per cent of the patrolmen circled choice C, which stated that when a patrolman appears at the Police Department Trial Room, he will probably be found guilty even when he has a good defense.

If these responses are an indication of the general attitude of members of the force toward their superior officers and the disciplinary system, what is the effect on morale? Either morale is low, or the interesting possibility is presented that there may be high morale even when members of an organization are deeply dissatisfied.

The Administrators

The higher echelons of large police forces assume a chauvinistic posture in order to defend their organization. They decry the lack of respect for law and order, and the difficulties created by the courts that seem to the police to be overprotective of criminals. At the same time police administrators are quick to take offense when criticized.

To maintain at all costs the virtue of their force, the administrators must sometimes do an abrupt about-face. For example, their most popular proof of police efficiency is an impressive statistical report. But if other statistics indicate a reduction in efficiency, they must somehow cushion the impact of figures. A good illustration of such a reversal occurred when the FBI published data for the first nine months of 1965 showing a 6.5 per cent rise for New York City crime over the comparable period of 1964. The New York *Times* reported that "a spokesman for the Police Department here declined to concede that this proved an 'unusually high' incidence of crime here,"[38] and quoted a deputy commissioner:

> [The statistics] were only three-quarters of the picture and reflect a crime bulge from the summer months.
> [The statistics] might show a drop at the end of the year and that could create a whole new average. Until you get the whole picture of the full year, you have only statistics.[39]

When statistics imply discredit, adminstrators either attack their source or devalue the statistics *per se*. In this case, since it is next to impossible for any police department to discredit

[38] New York *Times*, December 1, 1965, p. 95.
[39] *Ibid.*

the FBI, the statistics become the target. Police officials are not so lenient with critics of law enforcement.

When the Federal Narcotics Bureau was condemned for its treatment of suspects, the Bureau's answer was (according to Benjamin DeMott) a propaganda line hinting that "Any man who interests himself in the problem of 'unknown criminals' must have unsavory reasons for doing so."[40]

When civil rights groups criticized the FBI for its ambivalence in circumventing Mississippi segregationists, J. Edgar Hoover countered that Martin Luther King, Jr., was "the most notorious liar in the country."[41] Former New York City Police Commissioner Michael Murphy followed the same pattern in defending the action of his department in the civil rights disorders during the summer of 1964. Describing the frustration of the police who were "puzzled, bitter, and deeply resentful," he moved to the attack, asserting

that the public image of law enforcement—particularly as it involved the police—was unfairly "distorted and smeared today as never before in our history."

He said part of the picture was caused by "certain groups determined to weaken the democratic process."[42]

Probably the zenith of this administrative tropism was exemplified by Commissioner Vincent Broderick, the successor to Commissioner Murphy. Suffused by this extraordinary spirit of bureaucratic loyalty, he fought Mayor Lindsay himself, at the eventual cost of his job. The expected twist became apparent when the Commissioner elected publicly to interpret the mayor's call for a Civilian Review Board as an unwarranted political interference with the internal workings of the department, rather than to accept it as an ideal-

---

[40] "The Great Narcotics Muddle," *Harper's*, Vol. 214 (March 1962), p. 50.
[41] New York *Times*, November 20, 1964, p. 1.
[42] New York *Times*, August 23, 1964, p. 48.

istic innovation to honor a campaign pledge to promote better relations between the police and the city's minority groups.[43]

Police officials in this country envy the sacrosanct status enjoyed by Scotland Yard and the bobbies. But even these latter institutions seem to be losing their power to induce faith and silence criticism. In recent years Scotland Yard has had to cope with an England that can no longer be characterized as a nation of quiet, law-abiding citizens. The crime rate is rapidly increasing; the clearance rate is decreasing; sensational train robberies surpass TV thrillers; armed criminals kill policemen; race riots and teen-age gang rumbles signal social distress. Fleets of motorcycles roar through once peaceful communities. Traffic volume overwhelms the narrow streets of historic towns, and the police have antagonized the motoring public by traffic summons campaigns. Scandals have rocked the government.

These indications of disquiet are underlined by British press reports of bribery, brutality, forced confessions, racial discrimination, and illegally planted evidence. It is becoming difficult to attract capable recruits. When British police administrators submit annual reports, they are forced to defend certain obvious inadequacies. The British Police Superintendents' Association recently complained in a memorandum to the Home Secretary that

> Britain's Bobbies are being pilloried, bullied, restricted and increasingly unjustifiably criticized by members of the public in all walks of life . . . traditional British respect for the law [is] dwindling and . . . the police [can] not cope with a growing criminal element under present conditions.[44]

[43] It is notable that former Police Commissioners Francis Adams and Michael Murphy support Commissioner Broderick in his stand. New York *Times*, February 10, 1966, p. 1.
[44] New York *Times*, October 26, 1965, p. 13.

It is somewhat ironic, but nonetheless a testimonial to the efficiency and prestige of our own great police forces, that Roy Jenkins, the British Home Secretary, charged with responsibility for his country's police establishment, came to New York and Chicago on a police fact-finding mission.[45] It will certainly prove interesting to New York City police officials that there were more than nine thousand complaints lodged against Britain's police in 1965, and that as a result the influential *Economist* has proposed the formation of a civilian-dominated review board "on New York City's model."[46]

The Old-timer

Walking the streets, climbing stairs, lifting stretchers, and searching basements for armed criminals, the beat patrolman leads an active life that keeps him physically fit. It is a wrench the first time a rookie or youngster on his post calls him "Pop." Yet with fifteen years of service behind him, he is fast entering the circle of old-timers. In many of the personal interviews with policemen of this group, the men demonstrated a peculiar soul-searching type of introspection. Looking back over the years, they experienced a revulsion in reviewing all the distasteful acts of omission and commission in which they had participated.

They gradually assume the older statesman role and transmit the wisdom of the job to the new men. Seniority entitles them to the easier assignments, which allow them time to regale the younger men with endless reminiscences of the good old days when a cop could really be a cop. When

---

45 New York *Times*, October 1, 1966, p. 16.
46 *The Economist*, August 20, 1966, p. 711.

arguments occur, the split reveals a conflict of generations, each group paying allegiance to a different value system.

They recall with nostalgia, their early years on the job and often wonder at their former brashness. More and more their conversation becomes larded with the typical refrain of the aging, "When I was a rookie, things were different." Until this stage, the majority of the men talk confidently of retiring as soon as possible. However, at the approach of the twenty year retirement limit old-timers often begin to waver. What can the ordinary veteran policeman offer a prospective employer? His main talent, if he has one, is that of a low-level practitioner of applied psychology or sociology.

The typical position available to a former policeman is that of bank guard, night watchman, mail room clerk, or messenger. This demoralizing situation impels the policeman to stay with the force,[47] where he can be somewhat satisfied in knowing that he earns a salary many professional men would envy.

Even when they retire, most policemen preserve some connection with the force. Many former officers keep their revolvers, for which they must now obtain a permit. The retired patrolman's organization issues shields somewhat like those worn by active members of the force. Frequently, the retired men find new employment in security jobs requiring general police skills.

Significantly, disillusioned and threatened by his exposure to the job-hunter's world, the old-timer renews his commit-

[47] Appointments to the force are reported in the department's Annual Reports. Retirements can be found in the magazine *Spring 3100*. With the aid of these sources I traced a cohort of 1,674 policemen from appointment to the time of eligibility for retirement, covering a twenty-four-year period from 1941 until 1965. Counting all retirements except those for medical reasons, I found that more than fifty per cent of the cohort was still on the job at the beginning of 1965 when the cohort's average service was twenty-two and one-half years.

ment to the police occupation he probably deprecated as a recruit. The graph of cynicism patterns (see Appendix, Figure 1) over twenty years' service reflects this change among veterans approaching the twenty year milestone. Their degree of cynicism is consistently lower than that of men with less time on the job.

CHAPTER 4

Anomie *and* Cynicism

Seventy years ago, Emile Durkheim introduced the term *anomie*.[1] To the sociologist, *anomie* is a morbid condition of society characterized by the absence of standards, by apathy, confusion, frustration, alienation, and despair.[2] Other behavioral sciences designate *anomie* as anomia, alienation, self-estrangement, forlornness, anxiety, cultural desolation, or noögenic neurosis.[3]

Policemen with a philosophical or analytical bent are well aware of the threat of *anomie* in their world. They have their own idiosyncratic manner of describing it. One retired police officer, who was a supervisor in the Washington, D.C., Metropolitan Police Force, remarks:

> Among the problems that beset police officers, one concerns the emotional or psychological crisis which seems to come to every active and sincere policeman. . . .
> I have seen good men completely ruined by the hopeless

[1] Emile Durkheim, *The Division of Labor in Society, op. cit.;* Emile Durkheim, *Suicide* (Glencoe: The Free Press, 1951). See also, Robert K. Merton, "Social Structure and *Anomie*," in Robert K. Merton, *Social Theory and Social Structure* (Glencoe: The Free Press, 1957), pp. 131–194.

[2] For a sophisticated analysis of the sociological and psychological dimensions of *anomie*, see Herbert McClosky and John H. Schaar, "Psychological Dimensions of Anomy," *American Sociological Review*, Vol. 30 (February 1965), pp. 14–40.

[3] Viktor E. Frankl, *Man's Search for Meaning* (New York: Washington Square Press, 1964), pp. 160–170.

feeling. I have seen many become worthless to their Department, to their community and to themselves. Worse yet, I have seen some few turn crooked. . . . I don't know how much can be done about this problem in writing about it rather than talking about it with the men who are in danger, so that they would recognize this mental—perhaps it might even be called spiritual miasma that seems to hit too many good policemen. . . .

The second phase of this problem is much more serious and much more widespread than the loss suffered by resignation. It is an insidious thing, all the more dangerous because it is not at once evident and apparent. It is similar to cancer.[4]

The elements of this syndrome are loss of faith in people, of enthusiasm for the high ideals of police work, and of pride and integrity.

Anomie occurs particularly when the old values of a social system are being supplanted by a new code—exactly the case in the police organization. Seeking to wrest control from the old regime, the professionals are introducing a new ethic into the modern police force which is undermining old norms and loyalties. Caught between these contending forces, the policeman in the lower ranks feels uncertain of his position. The more professionalism becomes the predominant ethic, the greater each policeman's drive for advancement, and his disappointment at failure. There is also a parallel frustration when the public refuses to accord the force the professional status it desires.

According to Durkheim, the control exerted by law and morality creates a sense of social solidarity and is thus a

[4] Robert D. Dyas, "The Mental Miasma—A Police Personnel Problem," *Police*, Vol. 3 (July–August 1959), pp. 65–66. For an excellent analysis of the value conflicts that result in alienation, impotence, and "brass button" crime, see the work of another former police officer: Jacob Chwast, "Value-Conflicts in Law Enforcement," *Crime and Delinquency*, Vol. 11 (April 1965), pp. 151–161.

safeguard against *anomie*. At first impression it would appear
that above all other groups the police ought to be tied to the
law, but because they learn to manipulate it, the law can
become nothing but a means to an end. In performing his
special role in the social system, the policeman realizes that
for much of his time on duty he is above the law. Paradoxically, society has granted him the license to violate the law
in order to enforce it. He may kill where necessary, he may
destroy property and invade privacy; he may make arrests
merely on grounds of suspicion; he may disregard traffic regulations. The sense of power often corrupts him into a belief
that he is superior to the law.

The policeman is also set apart because he has the power
to regulate the life of others, a role symbolized by his distinctive weapons and uniform; likewise his constant dealing with
crime may encourage him to view policemen as superior to
the general race of men. As Westley indicates, it is difficult
for policemen to keep faith in mankind:

> The policeman's world is spawned of degradation, cor-
> ruption and insecurity. He sees men as ill-willed, exploitative,
> mean and dirty; himself a victim of injustice, misunderstood
> and defiled.[5]
> He tends to meet those portions of the public which are
> acting contrary to the law or using the law to further their
> own ends. He is exposed to public immorality. He becomes
> cynical. His is a society emphasizing the crooked, the weak
> and the unscrupulous. Accordingly his morality is one of
> expediency and his self-conception one of a martyr.[6]

[5] Westley, "The Police: A Sociological Study of Law, Custom, and
Morality," *op. cit.*, p. ii.
[6] *Ibid.*, p. 239. For a contemporary restatement of this theme in an excellent comparative study of police systems, see Michael Banton, *The Policeman in the Community* (New York: Basic Books, Inc., 1964), p. 169.

The Relation of Cynicism and Anomie

Robert K. Merton's widely acclaimed sociological model classifies the major types of adjustment to *anomie* as conformity, innovation, ritualism, retreatism, and rebellion. Another possibility prefigured by Nietzsche and Scheler, which Merton suggested in a footnote, is known as *ressentiment*, roughly translated as resentment, although in Merton's opinion, "no English word fully reproduces the complex of elements implied by the word *ressentiment*."[7]

This complex sentiment has three interlocking elements. First, diffuse feelings of hate, envy, and hostility; second, a sense of being powerless to express these feelings actively against the person or social stratum evoking them; and third, a continual re-experiencing of this impotent hostility. The essential point distinguishing *ressentiment* from rebellion is that the former does not involve a genuine change in values. *Ressentiment* involves a sour-grapes pattern which asserts merely that desired but unattainable objectives do not actually embody the prized values—[8]

In the police system the typical adaptation to *anomie* is cynicism. Like *ressentiment* it consists of diffuse feelings of hate[9] and envy, impotent hostility, and the sour-grapes pattern, and is used in this study to refer to a state of mind

[7] Robert K. Merton, *Social Theory and Social Structure, op. cit.*, p. 156, footnote 41.

[8] *Ibid.*, pp. 155–156.

[9] *Ressentiment* was clearly recognized in a study of the Syracuse police force. Commenting upon the police self-justification for their bitter attitudes, the authors found that, "This bitterness is reflected in this police force, in a catch phrase, 'I hate citizens.'" Elaine Cumming, Ian Cumming, and Laura Edell, "Policeman as Philosopher, Guide and Friend," *Social Problems*, Vol. 12 (Winter 1965), p. 285.

in which the *anomie* of the police organization as a whole is reflected in the individual policeman.

In the police world, cynicism is discernible at all levels, in every branch of law enforcement. It has also characterized police in other times and places. During the French Revolution and then under Napoleon, Joseph Fouché, the minister of police, concluded that with a few exceptions the world was composed of scoundrels, hypocrites, and imbeciles.[10] Many years later, reviewing the American police scene in 1939, Read Bain found that policemen were committed to the belief that the citizen was always trying "to get away with something," and that all men would commit crimes except for the fear of the police.[11]

In an interview conducted by the Center for the Study of Democratic Institutions, the late Chief William Parker of the Los Angeles Police Department was asked, "Are you inclined to be pessimistic about the future of our society?"

> I look back [he replied] over almost thirty-five years in the police service, thirty-five years of dealing with the worst that humanity has to offer. I meet the failures of humanity daily, and I meet them in the worst possible context. It is hard to keep an objective viewpoint. But it is also hard for me to believe that our society can continue to violate all the fundamental rules of human conduct and expect to survive. I think I have to conclude that this civilization will destroy itself, as others have before it. That leaves, then, only one question—when?[12]

[10] Louis Madelin, *Fouché 1759–1820* (Paris: Plon-Nourrit et Cie., 1903), p. 394.

[11] Read Bain, *op. cit.*, p. 451.

[12] *The Police: An Interview by Donald McDonald with William H. Parker, Chief of Police of Los Angeles, op. cit.*, p. 25. To the same effect see Michael Banton, *The Policeman in the Community, op. cit.*, p. 169. His view is that "The police departments have been demoralized by political control, poor leadership, and low rates of pay. The life of many districts seems competitive and raw; individuals pursue their own ends with little regard for public morality, and the policeman sees the ugly underside of outwardly respectable households and businesses. Small wonder then, that many American policemen are cynics."

A female store detective, with fifteen years of police experience to support her conclusions, states emphatically, "I am convinced that we are turning into a nation of thieves. I have sadly concluded that nine out of ten persons are dishonest."[13]

As noted before, it is possible to distinguish between two kinds of police cynicism. One is directed against life, the world, and people in general; the other is aimed at the police system itself.[14] The first is endemic to policemen of all ranks and persuasions—including the professionals. The second, common among patrolmen, is by definition excluded from the ideology of the professional policeman. The professional wants to transform and eventually control the system. This hope keeps him from cynicism.

Cynicism may be a by-product of *anomie* in the social structure; at the same time it may also prepare the way for personal *anomie* or anomia. Anxious over a personal failure, the individual policeman often disguises his feelings with a cynical attitude, and thus negates the value of the prize he did not attain. Frequently he includes in his cynicism all persons who still seek that prize or have succeeded in winning it, and, occasionally, deprecates the entire social system within which the failure occurred.

As the cynic becomes increasingly pessimistic and misanthropic, he finds it easier to reduce his commitment to the social system and its values. If the patrolman remains a

[13] Dorothy Crowe, "Thieves I Have Known," *Saturday Evening Post*, Vol. 234 (February 4, 1961), pp. 21, 78.

[14] An index of this attitude is the nearly universal desire to get out of uniform—the most visible sign of the police occupation. For this reason, there is not only a quest to become a detective, but also a refusal to wear the police uniform when off duty although a policeman has a right to do so. It is also revealed by the denigration of the police job. In a recently published study the author found that "For example, many of the Illinois police officers perceive their occupation to be a cause of ridicule to their children." John P. Clark, "Isolation of the Police: A Comparison of the British and American Situations," *Journal of Criminal Law, Criminology and Police Science*, Vol. 56 (September 1965), p. 313.

"loner," his isolation may lead to psychological *anomie* and even to suicide (see Table IV).

For the period 1950–1965 the average number of suicides in the New York City Police Department was 5, and its rate per 100,000 was 22.7. In contrast, the general suicide rate in New York City for the five-year period 1960–1964 was 11.5 per 100,000.[15] But this figure is derived from a population of 100,000 males and females in which the sex ratio (number of males per 100 females) was approximately 96.7. In addition, the suicide rate of males during that time was 1.7 times that of females.[16]

After the necessary adjustments are calculated, the suicide rate for males in the general New York City population is about 15 per 100,000. The average police rate of 22.7 is almost exactly fifty per cent more than this.

Anomie is not the inevitable outcome of police cynicism. Instead a policeman may be absorbed by the "delinquent" occupational subculture, dedicated to a philosophy of cynicism. This group may be deviant, but it is not anomic. It has a code of values and a clear, consistent ideology that function well in the police world. The members may be alienated from their former groups and goals, but they can be completely incorporated into this new reference group.

The third adaptation to cynicism is to overcome it, to regain commitment to the ideal of a decent and honorable career within the police force. Typically, there are two critical points in the advanced career of a policeman when he may discard cynicism. One crisis occurs when he considers retrospectively the many risks his career has involved. Fearing investigation, he may surrender his disaffection and resolve to do his job to the best of his ability. The second opportunity

---

[15] Personal communication from the Chief Medical Examiner's Office of New York City, September 20, 1965.

[16] *Ibid.*

TABLE IV
SUICIDES IN THE NEW YORK CITY POLICE DEPARTMENT[17]

Year	Number of Suicides	Size of Force Jan. 1 Each Year	Rate Per 100,000
1950	11	18,563	58
1951	3	19,016	16
1952	3	18,451	16
1953	6	18,762	31
1954	4	19,840	20
1955	8	20,080	37
1956	3	22,460	13
1957	4	23,193	17
1958	1	24,112	4
1959	8	23,636	34
1960	6	23,805	25
1961	5	23,515	20
1962	5	24,374	20
1963	3	24,827	11
1964	4	25,432	16
1965	7	25,897	26

Average Number 5.0   Average Rate 22.7
of Suicides   per 100,000
per Year

for reassessment comes when a man who is near retirement seeks another job and is often rebuffed. When this happens, a policeman's present situation understandably will seem more attractive to him.

The process leading to cynicism and *anomie* may be viewed as a continuum stretching from commitment at one end to *anomie* at the other, with cynicism as the critical intervening stage. Since police professionals are committed to the highest ideals of police work, they belong at the commitment end;

[17] SOURCE: Annual Reports of the New York City Police Department 1950–1965.

In computing the rate per 100,000, the size of the force for the whole year was obtained by adding the number on the rolls of the department January 1 of that year to the number on the rolls January 1 of the succeeding year, and then dividing by two.

the cynics around the opposite pole. The following model illustrates the typical stages that succeed one another as the policeman moves from commitment to cynicism and *anomie*.

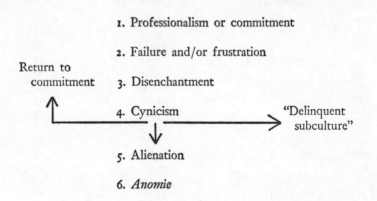

Differences in the patterns of cynicism are apparently related to a policeman's age and experience. The following classification scheme indicates that there is a succession of typical stages in the growth of cynicism that runs parallel to the occupational career.[18]

The preliminary stage, pseudo-cynicism, is recognizable among recruits at the training school. This attitude barely conceals the idealism and commitment beneath the surface.

The second stage, romantic cynicism, is reached in the first five years of the police career. The most idealistic young members of the force are precisely the ones who are most disillusioned by actual police work, and most vulnerable to this type of cynicism.

The third stage, aggressive cynicism, depends on the conjunction of individual cynicism and the subculture of cyni-

[18] I am indebted to Professor Joseph Bram of New York University for his help with this typology.

cism. It corresponds to *ressentiment* because resentment and hostility become obvious in this period, most prevalent at the ten year mark.

In the last few years of the police career, resigned cynicism replaces the former, more blatant type. This detachment may be passive and apathetic or express itself as a form of mellow if mild good will. It accepts and comes to terms with the flaws of the system.

Because these stages represent ideal types, there will probably be practical variations in style and degree.

Cynicism as an orientation to life depends for proof of its existence upon inferences drawn from human behavior. I have included descriptive material that indicates the likelihood of a correlation between police work and cynicism.

A more acceptable method is what Kenneth Clark has termed that of the "involved observer."[19] Because I was a policeman for more than twenty years, and have read a large portion of the police literature, I am convinced that there is a great deal of cynicism among my former colleagues.

Even so, the scientific method is most persuasive. The sociologist tries to emulate the rigor of the physical scientist: he observes and describes, collecting data; he classifies and compares, moving from the empirical to the conceptual. Thus he constructs hypotheses that cannot usually be tested by scientifically controlled experiment. The compromise solution is to prepare a questionnaire, most likely to evoke forthright responses, submit it to a well-chosen sample, and then analyze the results to see whether the hypotheses are substantiated. In this fashion research may be lifted to theory. I have utilized all these methods, emphasizing the last, formulating and testing several hypotheses in my study of police

[19] Kenneth Clark, *Dark Ghetto* (New York: Harper and Row, 1965), pp. xv–xviii.

cynicism. Although the study was completed toward the end of 1962, I believe that the tests of the following hypotheses are more than ever valid today.

1. For the first few years of a police career one's degree of cynicism will increase in proportion to his length of service, but it will tend to level off at some point between the fifth and tenth year of service. Generally, cynicism is learned as part of socialization into the police occupation, a process likely to take at least five years.

2. Newly appointed men will show less cynicism than more seasoned Police Academy recruits. In turn, the recruit group will be less cynical than the more experienced patrolmen: not only will the average degree of cynicism be lower, but there will be fewer cynics in the group.

3. Superior officers will be less cynical than patrolmen. According to our theory, cynicism is commonly a mode of adaptation to frustration. Cynicism should therefore vary positively according to the degree of failure and frustration. Men in the lower ranks have more reason to feel frustrated than do their superiors.

4. Among patrolmen, those with college educations will reveal a higher level of cynicism than other patrolmen because their expectations for promotion (still unfulfilled) were greater.

5. Patrolmen with preferred assignments (details) will be less cynical than other patrolmen.

6. Because foot patrolmen are of low status, they will be more cynical than patrolmen assigned to other duties.

7. Patrolmen who receive awards for meritorious duty will be less cynical. Patrolmen who are the subjects of departmental charges (complaints) will be more cynical.

8. Jewish patrolmen will be more cynical than non-Jewish patrolmen. Jewish tradition stresses that true success in life

lies in becoming a professional man. A Jewish policeman who remains a patrolman is thus a double failure: he did not become a doctor or lawyer, and he has been unable to rise from the low rank of patrolman.

9. When members of the force have served for seventeen or eighteen years, and are approaching retirement, they will exhibit less cynicism. When policemen near retirement search for employment outside the police system, they find opportunities distinctly limited. As a result, their appreciation of, and commitment to the police occupation revives.

10. Members of the Vice Squad will be more cynical than members of the Youth Division. The specific work situation within the organization plays its part in shaping attitudes.

11. Middle-class patrolmen will be less cynical than working-class patrolmen. Their receptivity to professionalism should insulate against cynicism. The middle-class ethic is more sympathetic to the ideas of professionalism than is the ideology of the working class.

So far we have tried to establish the relationship between the police system and cynicism. Is the system the only or even the principal source of cynicism? Perhaps police candidates were cynical, or at least vulnerable to cynicism, before becoming policemen. Does this possibility weaken our theory? In one sense anyone brought up in America, by the time he reaches his twenties, has internalized, along with the admirable qualities of Americans, a host of materialistic and cynical patterns of thought. We need only think of the distrust of "do-gooders," the anti-intellectualism, the "I'm from Missouri. Show me!" stance, the proverbial wisdom that there is a bit of larceny in everyone. Thus, we are all mixtures of idealism and cynicism. Other things being equal, we can expect the cynicism to be outweighed by the more attractive qualities. The question then arises, "Why is the police system with all its concentrated effort incapable, in so many cases, of dissipating that cynicism or encouraging the potent idealism?"

Still the lingering doubt persists. Is it not likely that there is something unusual about an individual who chooses to become a policeman? If he is not clearly cynical, is he not typically authoritarian? And, then once more, is it not true that authoritarianism and cynicism are strongly connected?

CHAPTER 5

Authoritarian Police Personality

Which is the more important determinant of behavior, the internal dynamics of personality emphasized by psychologists, or the external pressures of the occupational role, stressed by sociologists? The psychological view, insofar as it applies to the police, echoes public sentiment. In an interview with Chief William H. Parker of Los Angeles, Dean Donald McNamara of the College of Journalism of Marquette University stated,

> An attitude I find frequently among well intentioned people is that the police officer is sometimes a frustrated dictator who is attracted to the police service in order to give vent to his aggressive or neurotic feelings.[1]

In a study using policemen as the control group, David Rapaport advanced the opinion that

> This adjustment as a patrolman may have been, in many cases, an effort of sublimation or the choice of a mode of life where their restlessness or aggression found a socially acceptable form of expression.[2]

The theory of occupational choice formulated by Eli Ginzberg and his colleagues proposes that personality needs play an important part in the choice of a career.[3] But the

[1] *The Police: An Interview by Donald McDonald with William H. Parker, Chief of Police of Los Angeles, op. cit.*, p. 12.
[2] David Rapaport, *op. cit.*, Vol. 1, p. 28.
[3] Eli Ginzberg, Sol Ginsburg, Sidney Axelrad, and John Herma, *Occupational Choice: An Approach to a General Theory* (New York: Columbia University Press, 1951).

theory does not say that only one type of personality chooses one job. Obviously different needs are satisfied by the same job and in most occupations there is no indication that one type of personality predominates. Anne Roe suggests that there is a correlation between personality and choice of work, while restricting its application to a few unspecified specialized occupations.

> No true comprehensive work has been done with person-ality tests as such in the field of occupational psychology. There are many studies of particular groups by personality inventories, and a few with projective and other techniques. Although the evidence is not extensive, there nevertheless seems to be no doubt that some specialized occupations, at least, do attract persons who resemble each other in some personality characteristics.[4]

In *The Psychology of Careers*, Donald Super is equally cautious, straddling the fence on both sides.

> In closing this discussion of the relationship between per-sonality and vocational development, it is important to point out that any conclusions reached on this subject at present are highly tentative. . . .
>
> 1. Personality traits seem to have no clear-cut and practical significant differential relationship to vocational preference, entry, success, or satisfaction.
> 2. It seems possible that, if occupations are sufficiently nar-rowly and precisely defined, for example in terms of func-tional specialties within an occupation, significant personality differences in occupational groups may be found. Perhaps some will be found which are so highly structured that only individuals with certain traits are successful or satisfied in them. . . .[5]

[4] Anne Roe, *Psychology of Occupations* (New York: John Wiley and Sons, Inc., 1956), p. 80.
[5] Donald Super, *The Psychology of Careers* (New York: Harper and Brothers, 1957), pp. 240–241.

The relation between personality and occupational choice remains an open question.

Nor do matters improve when we turn to authoritarianism. The term refers to a collection of traits whose permutations and combinations are astronomical. To complicate the matter, some of the qualities that are blended together in authoritarian persons cancel each other out. For example, aggression and submission are both responses consistent with authoritarianism. The concept shares some of the mystery common to such well-known personality dimensions delineated in psychoanalytical doctrine as the unconscious, the id, the super-ego, the libido, the Oedipus complex, racial archetypes, sado-masochism, etc. Behavior that seems to indicate one tendency may, on Freud's authority, signify its exact opposite. For example, the Freudian may classify a philanderer as a latent homosexual.

Equally ambiguous is the connection between an occupational role and the person who fills it. Does the occupational authoritarian necessarily possess an authoritarian personality? The confusion in definitions and boundaries is implicit in the discussion of police authoritarianism.

What other civilian occupation can be likened in this respect to police work? The legal authority to use force is for the police perhaps their principal technique in fighting crime. During the training period the dictum "Take charge of the situation" is later underscored by the use of the revolver and the nightstick. For the most part police duty consists of the following directives: Arrest! Summons! Warn! Regulate! Direct! Disperse! Prevent! Use necessary force! Hold for investigation! Take into custody! The tough cop is the sort who can employ the primary police directives to warn, issue summonses, investigate, take into custody, make arrests, and use necessary force. In a well-conceived theory of authoritarianism, Don Stewart and Thomas Hoult combine the concept of authoritarianism with that of role prescriptions. The example of the police authoritarian is used to illustrate their thesis.

> (e) it includes the possible existence of "occupational authoritarians" (physicians, policemen, army personnel, priests, and the like), who may exhibit authoritarian traits as an occupational necessity and who therefore may have high F scores even though they happen to be products of, say, a loving and democratic family, which, according to psychoanalytic theory, produces non-authoritarians.[6]

Any discussion of authoritarianism must turn to the classic work on the subject—*The Authoritarian Personality*, which grew out of a conference on racial and religious prejudice called by the American Jewish Committee in 1944. The scientific investigation of anti-Semitism led to ethnocentrism, and ended with the more inclusive concept of authoritarianism that contains nine main clusters of variables:

a. Conventionalism.
b. Authoritarian submission.
c. Authoritarian aggression.
d. Anti-intraception.
e. Superstition and stereotypy.
f. Power and toughness.
g. Destructiveness and cynicism.
h. Projectivity.
i. Sex.[7]

Basic to this study was a series of interviews incorporating

[6] Don Stewart and Thomas Hoult, "A Social Psychological Theory of the Authoritarian Personality," *American Journal of Sociology*, Vol. 65 (November 1959), p. 278.

[7] T. W. Adorno, Else Frenkel-Brunswik, Daniel J. Levinson, and R. Nevitt Sanford, *The Authoritarian Personality* (New York: Harper and Brothers, 1950), p. 228.

projective material from the Thematic Apperception Test. In addition to the standard pictures the research group included a photograph of a policeman facing a man in a white T-shirt. This was "commonly interpreted as a suspect caught by the police," but those ranking high in authoritarianism "often reject[ed] the suspect and identif[ied] more closely with the police authority."[8]

The F (Fascist) scale by which to measure authoritarianism was a product of the research. A factor analysis of the F scale items by Robert Krug produced "six reasonably stable factors" almost identical to the original clusters. These factors were labeled:

1. conventionalism,
2. cynicism,
3. aggression,
4. superstition and stereotypy,
5. projectivity, and
6. good versus bad people.

Factor 3 was composed of two main themes, sex and aggression.[9] Krug's description of Factor 2 is of particular interest.

> Factor 2 is less than crystal clear. The dominant theme seems to be a negative attitude toward the present: a "things are going to pot" view. The factor is tentatively termed cynicism.[10]

Some other features of the authoritarian personalities de-

---

[8] *Ibid.*, picture 6 opposite p. 509, and p. 527.

[9] Robert E. Krug, "An Analysis of the F Scale: 1. Item Factor Analysis," *Journal of Social Psychology*, Vol. 53 (1961), pp. 288, 291.

[10] *Ibid.*, pp. 287–288. Another factor analysis study of *anomie*, authoritarianism, and prejudice found a common substructure for all three. It was "labeled as a *Weltanschauung* which is negative in nature." See Edward L. McDill, "*Anomie*, Authoritarianism, Prejudice," *Social Forces*, Vol. 39 (March 1961), p. 245.

serve mention because they are all made manifest in the occupational role of the policeman.

Conventionalism is defined as the "rigid adherence to conventional middle-class values."[11] Although the typical policeman has a working-class background, the occupational role requires that he display a middle-class behavior and ideology partially because he is supposed to keep the public conduct as nearly conventional as possible.[12]

In the New York City Police Department, which sets the standard for other police forces, Rule 53 of the guide directs recruits to "wear a conservative business suit with matching coat and trousers"[13] when it is necessary to dress in mufti. Rule 64 states that "hair must be trimmed in a conservative style. High pompadours, and long side-burns are prohibited. . . . Recruits must be clean shaven with no mustache."[14] Together with all other members of the force, recruits are required to "avoid behavior that would tend to bring adverse criticism of the department."[15]

During the nine month probationary period, a recruit may be dropped at any time at the discretion of the Commissioner, so long as the dismissal is not arbitrary and capricious. There is a case on record in which a probationary patrolman was discharged because the Police Department did not think highly enough of the woman the recruit was courting. It was charged that "his association with [her] brought, or tended to bring, adverse criticism of the Police Department."[16] In this case the Supreme Court of New

[11] T. W. Adorno, *et al.*, *op. cit.*, p. 228.

[12] Skolnick hesitated to accept the concept of police authoritarian personality. He thought it "preferable to call the policeman's a conventional personality." See Jerome H. Skolnick, *op. cit.*, p. 61.

[13] New York City Police Department, *Recruits Issue Material* (New York: The Police Academy, 1958), p. 23.

[14] *Ibid.*, p. 24.

[15] New York City Police Department, *Rules and Procedures*, Chapter 2, paragraph 63.2 (1960).

[16] New York *Times*, August 8, 1964, p. 8.

York State overruled the Police Commissioner, and the petitioner was reinstated.

Even after the probationary period is over, members of the force may be charged for past transgressions. A young, unmarried, honor policeman with two years of service was threatened with dismissal because he allegedly had sexual intercourse with an unmarried woman during his probationary period. It was charged that he had "engaged in conduct tending to bring adverse criticism to the department."[17] At the trial his defense attorney, a former policeman himself, noted that "if chastity is to become a new requirement for policemen, cops will have to be chosen from choir boys."[18]

Members of the force have a morbid fear that someone will write a letter of complaint to the Commissioner about them. A strong belief persists that even those that are obviously the work of cranks are thoroughly investigated. Therefore, most policemen when off duty try to conceal their occupation and avoid conflicts of any nature.

Reading like an advertisement for a successful police investigator, the description of projectivity in *The Authoritarian Personality* emphasizes that

> preoccupation with "evil forces" in the world [is] shown by his readiness to think about and to believe in the existence of such phenomena as wild erotic excesses, plots and conspiracies.[19]

A good detective must be suspicious; he needs the intuitive ability to sense plots and conspiracies on the basis of embryonic evidence. Specially trained experts in the Los Angeles and New York City Police Departments use computers to perform factor analysis on data obtained from seemingly unrelated crimes, attempting to detect a pattern indicative of

[17] New York *Post*, May 10, 1965, p. 3.
[18] *Ibid.*
[19] T. W. Adorno, *et al.*, *op. cit.*, p. 240.

some vast conspiracy. The existence of syndicates like the Mafia and Cosa Nostra does much to convince the police that their vigilance alone prevents such organizations from destroying the United States.

Suspicion becomes second nature to many policemen. Cynical as they are, they can at the same time be very moralistic about others' behavior. Their common complaint is that "nowadays there is no respect for law and order." Projectivity makes them enemies of Communists and unspecified "do-gooders." At the same time it strengthens their attraction to reactionary political groups.

Political conservatism has been highly correlated with authoritarianism, and the police usually occupy the conservative band of the political spectrum.[20] A generation ago policemen belonged to organizations like the Christian Front; today they are rumored to swell the ranks of the John Birch Society.[21]

The Birch Society made a special effort to recruit policemen members by displaying auto bumper signs ("Support Your Local Police") and by conducting political campaigns against civilian review boards in Massachusetts and New York.[22] One New York City patrolman, a chapter leader of the Birch Society, placed an advertisement in the local newspaper proclaiming that "policemen join the John Birch Society because we know, among other things, that to be a

[20] For example, in a study of a police force in California, "it was clear that a Goldwater type of conservatism was the dominant political and emotional persuasion of police." See Jerome H. Skolnick, *op. cit.*, p. 61.

[21] New York *Post*, July 9, 1965. According to the New York *Times* November 8, 1965, p. 1, two well-known police figures have become public speakers for the Birch Society. The former police chief of Salt Lake City, W. Cleon Skousen, "author of *The Naked Communist* and other right-wing writings, was to speak on Law and Order: Civil Disobedience." And Sheriff James Clark of Selma, Alabama, was scheduled to "tell his version of the civil rights struggle at Selma this year." A former Newark police detective is the coordinator for the Birch Society in Central New Jersey. See New York *Times*, April 20, 1966, p. 34.

[22] New York *Times*, March 24, 1966, p. 35.

member of the John Birch Society is to be for God, Family
and Country, [and that membership in the society makes us]
better police-officers and better Americans for so doing."[23]
The Society itself estimates that it has five hundred members
in the New York City Police Department. A departmental
investigation into the question of Birch Society membership
was undertaken shortly after the advertisement appeared, but
it seems to have faded away without published results.

The Birch Society self-image of patriotic Americans was
denounced by Arnold Forster, general counsel to the Anti-
Defamation League of B'nai B'rith.

> The John Birch Society is a political organization, that . . .
> fosters hatred and prejudice against racial and religious
> groups and . . . a policeman's membership in it interferes
> with the performance of his duties.[24]

To discuss this question intelligently we must first know
the laws and rules pertaining to political activities by policemen, some of which are forbidden:

New York State Penal Law, Section 756, Subdivision 3

Any person who, being a police commissioner or an officer or member of any police force in this state:

3. Contributes any money, directly or indirectly, to, or
solicits, collects or receives any money for, any political
fund, or joins or becomes a member of any political club,
association, society or committee.

Is guilty of a misdemeanor.

New York City Charter, Chapter 18, Section 439

Political Activities Forbidden

Members of the police force shall not contribute any
moneys, directly or indirectly, to any political fund, or

---

[23] Staten Island *Advance*, March 7, 1966, p. 9.
[24] New York *Times*, March 19, 1966, p. 15.

any fund intended to effect an increase in their emoluments, or join or be or become a member of any political organization, but nothing herein shall be construed to deny to such members any right afforded by section eleven hundred thirty-four.

The New York City Police Department Rules and Procedures also cover this subject in Chapter 2:

Rule 8.0

The right of every member of the force to vote, to entertain political or partisan opinions and to express them freely when they do not concern the immediate discharge of his duties is deemed inviolate. But no member of the force may belong to a political club or take active part in the nomination or election of candidates for public office.

Rule 11.0

A member of the force shall not affiliate with or become a member of any organization if such affiliation or membership would in any way interfere with or prevent him from performing police duty.

Rule 14.0

A member of the department, except in the discharge of official duty, shall not knowingly associate or have dealings with any person or organization advocating or instrumental in fostering hatred or prejudice against or oppression of any racial or religious group.

Rule 63.2

Members of the department shall carefully avoid behavior that would tend to bring adverse criticism of the department. Their conduct, whether on or off duty, shall be such as to merit the confidence and respect of the people.

There are, therefore, several grounds on which police membership in the Birch Society might constitute a violation of law or police regulations. These depend on the resolution of the following questions:

1. Is the John Birch Society a political organization?
2. Is the John Birch Society a subversive organization?
3. Does the John Birch Society foster hatred or prejudice against any racial or religious group?
4. Does membership in the John Birch Society interfere with or prevent the performance of police duty?
5. Does membership in the John Birch Society constitute such behavior that would tend to bring adverse criticism of the department, or that would reduce the confidence and the respect of the people?

A New York State Joint Legislative Committee on Election Laws after conducting hearings into the nature of the John Birch Society found

> that the John Birch Society was a political organization and that any policeman who belonged to it violated the Penal Law.[25]

This finding was not binding on the New York City Police Department since it operates under the authority of the New York City Charter. Both Mayor Lindsay and Commissioner Leary have publicly condemned the Birch Society and deplored the fact that policemen were among its members. It is a testimonial to their concern for legality that the question was resubmitted for consideration by the New York City Corporation Counsel, J. Lee Rankin, who held that the Birch Society was not a political organization within the meaning of the State Penal Code and the New York City Charter.[26] The Commissioner thereupon took the position that he

25 New York *Times*, May 10, 1966, p. 1.
26 New York *Times*, May 28, 1966, p. 25.

can't do anything about it [because] prohibition by me of membership would appear to be an unwarranted interference of the constitutional right of association.[27]

Police membership in the John Birch Society is therefore legal. At present, it is unlikely that the Birch Society will be placed on the Attorney General's list of subversive organizations—not as long as it proclaims itself against communism and for "God, Family and Country." There is insufficient evidence to prove the serious charge that the Birch Society fosters hatred and prejudice against racial or religious groups, nor can it be demonstrated, except by inference, that membership interferes with police duty.

The last question poses a problem. For many reasons, Jews suspect that behind the patriotic stance of the Birch Society lurks bitter anti-Semitism, the trademark of the radical right. Negroes distrust the Birch Society because it supports segregation and white supremacy.[28] Together, Negroes and Jews in New York City number more than three million persons—forty per cent of the population. Without question, these groups will criticize the department if a sizable number of policemen join the Birch Society. Does adverse criticism by three million Negroes and Jews count as the kind of adverse criticism envisaged in Rule 63.2?[29]

It is likely that police membership in the Birch Society will increase. In the first place, the ideologies of both organizations are to some degree similar. The Birch Society also offers policemen potential leverage to resist and possibly to nullify the advances made by minority groups at the expense of the police.

[27] *Ibid.*

[28] For example, see New York *Times,* November 8, 1965, p. 1, and April 20, 1966, p. 34.

[29] Compare the case of the patrolman whose girl friend did not meet the approval of the department. See pp. 108–109.

Distrust and suspicion, so deeply imbued in policemen, often alienate those agencies upon whom they depend: the press and the courts. The police need the support of the press in order to clarify their attitudes for the public. They need the cooperation of the courts because police arrests must be validated by conviction in court. Yet the police often take pains to offend journalists and judges by impugning their motives.[30]

In England more than two-thirds of the policemen interviewed by the Royal Commission on the Police thought that the press was responsible for the increasing public hostility toward them. They produced press cuttings that depicted policemen in an unfavorable light.[31] The Royal Commission defended the press in the following manner:

> The defaulting policeman, like the defaulting parson or schoolteacher, is "news"; and stories of the prosecution and conviction of policemen are frequently given prominence in the press. We do not think that the reputation of the police service stands or falls by the occasional sensational reporting of allegations against a particular policeman.[32]

Police opinion in America generally distrusts the newspapers. O. W. Wilson, Superintendent of the Chicago Police Department, states the case baldly.

> The press, the literature, and the case law are primarily directed at incidents that tend to discredit the police. Small wonder that those who read the papers or research the literature and case law conclude that the police are evil.[33]

[30] In the cynicism study (see Appendix) more than eighty-five per cent of the patrolmen thought that the newspapers enjoyed giving an unfavorable slant to police news.

[31] Great Britain, *Final Report of the Royal Commission on the Police* (London: Her Majesty's Stationery Office, 1962), pp. 104, 118.

[32] *Ibid.*, p. 118.

[33] O. W. Wilson, "Police Authority in a Free Society," *Journal of Criminal Law, Criminology and Police Science*, Vol. 54 (June 1963), p. 176. Westley stressed the fact that the police regarded themselves as a minority

Articles in police journals reiterate this theme; for example,

> Police departments seem to be one of the favorite targets of the press. Small things are made large, any little slip gets memorialized on the front page, and given a big scandal, the papers will spend weeks in an ecstasy of editorials.[34]

Do the facts justify these views? Careful content analysis of all police news appearing in the New York *Times* and the New York *Daily News* during the six month period from April to October 1958 revealed that, if anything, the press is rather sympathetic to the police.[35]

> In the opinion of this writer, one who read the *Daily News* exclusively would probably have an emotional impression of [the police as] a large group of individuals engaged in an exciting and glamorous job. . . .
> Reports of sensational arrests tend to obtain the admiration of readers of the *Daily News* for the individual policemen and for the police department as a whole. Stories of police activity categorized as service tend to create a warmly favorable opinion of policemen in the readers' minds.[36]

> The New York *Times'* presentation tends, in this writer's opinion, to create in its readers attitudes favorable to law enforcement, willingness to cooperate with the police, and confidence in the police force.[37]

---

group. Commissioner Michael Murphy of the New York City Police Department reiterated: "the police officer, too, belongs to a minority group . . ." (Speech delivered at a meeting of the Engineers' Club in New York City, April 28, 1964). The English police also feel that they are a minority group. See Ben Whitaker, *The Police* (Harmondsworth: Penguin Books Ltd., 1964), p. 131.

[34] Richard H. Blum, "The Problems of Being a Police Officer," *Police*, Vol. 5 (January–February 1961), p. 36.

[35] Benjamin Stalzer, "Press Portrayal of the New York City Police Department with a Content Analysis of the New York *Daily News* and the New York *Times* of April 1, 1958, to October 1, 1958" (unpublished Master's dissertation, Bernard M. Baruch School of Business and Public Administration, The City College of the College of the City of New York, 1961). Mr. Stalzer was a police captain in the New York City Police Department at the time he made this study.

[36] *Ibid.*, pp. 133–134.

[37] *Ibid.*, p. 135.

Policemen consider the court system the most uncoopera-
tive agency.[38] O. W. Wilson concurs with this attitude:

Highly intelligent people . . . conceive the police as a
potential instrument of tyranny. . . .
These citizens, as protectors of liberty and freedom, then
align themselves against the police without giving attention
to the cost of criminal depredations.
Decisions of our courts tend to reflect these hostilities
against the police in a continuing stream of opinions restricting the police in their authority to enforce the law and protect the lives and property of our citizens.[39]

Criminal lawyers are sometimes in diametrical disagreement. In December 1961, a New York City attorney submitted an affidavit to the Court of General Sessions, stating
that it is "impossible to get a fair trial" for a defendant in
Gamblers Court because the magistrates "almost automatically accept the word of a police officer against that of a
defendant or his witnesses."[40] Five months later when the
police conviction rate in gambling cases had been drastically
reduced, the Police Department "launched a secret investigation of the City's gambling courts" on the theory that "direct
'fixes' [were being arranged] between individual judges and
gamblers, or the judges might be paying off political debts."[41]
The police probers concealed tape recorders, and compiled
dossiers on judges. A newspaper reporter familiar with the
facts concluded that

The situation is explosive. Court observers said today its
repercussions are likely to rock the judiciary and create a

[38] There was one statement on this subject included in the cynicism
questionnaire. Forty per cent of the patrolmen agreed that too often
policemen are treated like criminals when they take the witness stand in
court (see Appendix).
See also New York *Times*, September 5, 1965, p. 48, in which the principal
article on the page is entitled, "Court's Decisions Frustrate Police."
[39] O. W. Wilson, "Police Authority in a Free Society," *op. cit.*, p. 177.
[40] New York *Herald Tribune*, December 15, 1961, p. 20.
[41] New York *World Telegram*, May 10, 1962, p. 1.

considerable amount of ill will between the courts and the Police Department.[42]

Anti-intraception is an attitude which

easily leads to a devaluation of the human and an overvaluation of the physical object; when it is most extreme, human beings are looked upon as if they were physical objects to be coldly manipulated.[43]

The anti-intraceptive individual "is afraid of what might be revealed if he, or others, should look closely at himself. He is therefore against 'prying.' "[44] The police authoritarian relies heavily on the manipulation of people; and although it is his job to pry into the affairs of others, he opposes any investigation into the secrets of the police system.[45] Like the anti-intraceptive person policemen exhibit an antipathy to psychology and sociology as indicated above.[46]

The police system transforms a man into the special type of authoritarian personality required by the police role. No matter what kind of person he was before joining, the system's brilliant success in creating authoritarian personalities is sometimes a source of serious trouble. Since the policeman feels justified and righteous in using power and toughness to perform his duties, he feels like a martyr when he is charged with brutality and abuse of power.

This sentiment probably prompted 5,600 New York City

[42] Ibid.

[43] T. W. Adorno, et al., op. cit., p. 235.

[44] Ibid.

[45] See William A. Westley, "Secrecy and the Police," Social Forces, Vol. 34 (1956), pp. 254–257. He found that "the maintenance of secrecy is a fundamental rule" of the police.

[46] The policeman becomes anti-intraceptive as he gains experience on the job probably because of a sense of group loyalty which makes him see the researcher who is conducting a study as an enemy. On the other hand, police candidates just appointed and not yet brainwashed may be high on intraception. See Joseph D. Matarazzo, et al., "Characteristics of Successful Policemen and Firemen Applicants," Journal of Applied Psychology, Vol. 48 (1964), p. 128.

policemen at a Holy Name Society Communion Breakfast to cheer William Buckley, the 1965 Conservative candidate for mayor of New York, when he "praised the restraint of the police in Selma, Alabama, and criticized the civil rights marchers."[47] Buckley echoed the automatic response of police spokesmen to critics when he concluded "Men who rail unthinkingly against policemen tend to have a relationship with revolutionaries."[48]

The strong sexual component supposedly typical of authoritarian personalities can be separated into three different dimensions: (1) a positive emphasis upon sexuality and virility as the *sine qua non* of a real man; (2) an ambivalence toward, and vague distrust of, women; (3) the possibility of latent homosexuality related to a fear of masculine inadequacy.

Modern literature lends credence to the belief in police *machismo*. Popular stereotypes of the policeman include the dumb cop, the patrolman with the incomprehensible brogue, the traffic officer brandishing the summons book—and the Casanova.

The police are a subculture of males in the prime of life. The precinct has about it a "locker room" aura, pervaded by a strong erotic quality. Erving Goffman considers this development inevitable in male service occupations.

> And when we study service occupations, especially lowly ones, inevitably we find that practitioners have anecdotes to tell about the time they or one of their colleagues redefined the service relation into a sexual one (or had it redefined for them). Tales of such aggressive redefinitions are a significant part of the mythology not only of particular occupations but also of the male subculture generally.[49]

[47] New York *Times,* April 5, 1965, p. 35.
[48] *Ibid.*
[49] Erving Goffman, *The Presentation of Self in Everyday Life* (Garden City: Doubleday & Co., Inc., 1959), p. 194.

The policeman does well for himself in the battle of the sexes. His rugged physique, natty military uniform, sexually symbolic occupational tools, and aura of power combine to make him a figure of virility and undoubtedly have raised his status as a potential husband. Twenty years ago the policeman was a proper boyfriend for the housemaid; today he can successfully aspire to a teacher or a nurse.

In the performance of duty, patrolmen are subjected to greater sexual temptations than members of other occupations. Voyeurism is built into the police job; it is a legitimate function, an aspect of the license and guilty knowledge which may be the basic criterion of a professional occupation.[50]

The sexual emphasis of police work is frequently revealed by the nicknames that are given to men with unusual endowments, such as Mattress Mike, Harry the Horse, and Sexy Rexy.[51] Even policemen who are only average specimens are quick to defend their honor against any imputation of the lack, or loss, of virility.

While policemen have the greatest affection for women, as women, they react with hostility and resigned despair when they must face women as police clientele. One widely used training manual now in its sixth printing warns that

> Since most policemen present a good appearance in a uniform, they are likely to attract women. Some women may try to force their attentions on you. Every police department has had experience with this type of woman. Encouraging this type can result only in trouble.[52]

Women involved in police incidents are generally considered to be unreasonable, quick to take offense, even

[50] Everett C. Hughes, "The Study of Occupations," in *Sociology Today, op. cit.*, pp. 447–452.

[51] John M. Murtagh and Sara Harris, *Cast the First Stone* (New York: McGraw-Hill Book Co., 1957), p. 247.

[52] Richard L. Holcomb, *Police and the Public* (Springfield: Charles C. Thomas, 1964), p. 13.

dangerous. Under the heading, "Women to Watch Out For," the training manual offers this advice to the practical policeman:

> Public opinion certainly frowns upon striking a woman no matter what the provocation may be. Many of the women you arrest realize this and will go to any lengths to get you angry enough to use force.
>
> Such women are notoriously unfair in their practices when it comes to fighting policemen. They know more about a well placed knee or what they can do with the heel of a slipper than is ever taught in a course in Judo. They know more vile names than many men.
>
> For these reasons you should be particularly careful when you are making such an arrest and plan your arrest well. Try to have help if you possibly can.[53]

This distrust of women seems to be historical and institutionalized among men working with the law. A Florentine statute of the thirteenth century (1294) gives this quaintly ambiguous warning: "Women are a sex to be looked upon as most dangerous in disturbing the course of justice."[54]

Of all occupations the police are apparently most free from the taint of homosexuality. The merest hint of effeminacy would absolutely bar a candidate from appointment to the force, and after the probationary period, any sign of homosexuality would lead to his immediate dismissal or forced resignation. The idea of police homosexuality is difficult to credit, but the police inspire such feelings of hostility that their detractors often interpret their behavior in this light. The scientist takes a middle road, neither rejecting nor accepting the possibility of police homosexuality.

Two statements on the F scale (which measures authori-

[53] Ibid., p. 13.
[54] Marvin E. Wolfgang, "Socio-Economic Factors Related to Crime and Punishment in Renaissance Florence," Journal of Criminal Law, Criminology and Police Science, Vol. 47 (September–October 1956), p. 317.

tarianism) are particularly relevant. Strong agreement with them was characteristic of high authoritarians, and by implication, of latent homosexuality.

> 31. Homosexuality is a particularly rotten form of delinquency and ought to be severely punished.
> 75. Sex crimes, such as rape and attacks on children, deserve more than mere imprisonment; such criminals ought to be publicly whipped.[55]

Policemen do exhibit an exaggerated hatred of sex offenders. In Westley's study he found that for policemen, sex cases represent

> an area of intolerance and of difficulties. Their intolerance arises perhaps from personal definitions, from public approval of intolerance. It manifests itself in extremely rough treatment of the offender, the "take him out in the alley and beat him up" attitude.[56]

A randomly arranged list of the most disliked segments of the police clientele was submitted to the sample of policemen in the cynicism study (see Appendix). Table V reveals that homosexuals were the second most disliked group.

In a pilot study, I asked twenty-two patrolmen to rank sixteen major crimes from most to least serious. The crime they adjudged most serious was carnal abuse, which usually involves sexual fondling of a child, short of sexual intercourse. It is either a misdemeanor or a felony depending on the age of the child, but in the opinion of this small sample of policemen, such an attack on a child merited more severe punishment than murder or kidnaping, which at that time called for the death penalty.

According to the theory of *The Authoritarian Personality*,

---

[55] T. W. Adorno, *et al.*, *op. cit.*, p. 240.
[56] Westley, "The Police: A Sociological Study of Law, Custom, and Morality," *op. cit.*, p. 116.

TABLE V

POLICE ATTITUDES TOWARD THEIR CLIENTELE
N=186.   1 is most disliked.   16 is least disliked.

1. Cop-fighter
2. Homosexual
3. Drug addict
4. Chronic letterwriter
5. Annoying drunk
6. Bookie
7.5 Gang of juveniles
7.5 Prostitute
9. Known criminal
10. Motorcycle group
11. Psycho
12. Motorist who double parks
13. Peddler
14. Woman complainant
15. Bohemian
16. Minority group member

persons with high authoritarianism emphasize sexuality, possess ambivalent attitudes toward women, and condemn sex offenders, qualities supposedly attributable to latent homosexuality disguised by projection or reaction formation.[57] The police exhibit these traits as part of their occupational ideology. Does this imply that policemen may be latent homosexuals?[58]

Alfred C. Kinsey adds some circumstantial evidence about men, who like policemen, have only high school educations.

The number of males who have any homosexual experience after the onset of adolescence (the accumulative incidence) is highest in the group that enters high school but never goes beyond in its educational career. In that group 55 per cent of the males who are still single by 30 years of

[57] T. W. Adorno, et al., op. cit., p. 241.
[58] Army men are often studied in terms similar to those used here. See the discussion of latent homosexuality in Henry Elkin "Aggressive and Erotic Tendencies in Army Life," op. cit.

age have had the experience of being brought to climax through a physical contact with another male.[59]

Prior to the publication of *The Authoritarian Personality*, Kinsey also found that rates of homosexuality were highest among those males who most fiercely condemned homosexuals.

> The highest incidences of the homosexual, however, are in the group which most often verbalizes its disapproval of such activity. This is in the group that goes into high school but never beyond in its educational career. These are the males who most often condemn the homosexual, most often ridicule and express disgust for such activity, and most often punish other males for their homosexuality. And yet, this is the group which has the largest amount of overt homosexual activity.[60]

Would a man with one or more such experiences be classified as a homosexual? Or is it a question of the latent potential that may never be observable to anyone, or even known consciously by the person himself? Are policemen logical candidates for inclusion in the group described by Kinsey which, he says, constitutes nearly fifty per cent of the male population? In education and ideology, policemen fit Kinsey's pattern; and police duty does bring them into contact with homosexuals, who seem to be attracted to policemen.[61]

[59] Alfred C. Kinsey, Wardell B. Pomeroy, and Clyde E. Martin, *Sexual Behavior in the Human Male* (Philadelphia: W. B. Saunders Co., 1948), pp. 627–629.

[60] *Ibid.*, p. 384.

[61] To novelists any all-male society—a school for boys, a prison for men, the Army, and the police force—is a natural setting for a homosexual friendship. Such writers, whatever the sincerity of their commitment to art, often introduce some hard-core pornography into their work. Apparently, when a symbol of power and virility like the policeman succumbs to homosexuality in the pages of a book, the inversion of roles excites the cognoscenti of perversion. Thus it is not unusual to find literary allusions to cases where policemen reportedly become involved with homosexuals.

Intriguing evidence of policemen's lack of masculinity was presented by Terman and Miles in 1936 (see Introduction).[62] While studying policemen and firemen in California, the two psychologists discovered to their surprise that the thirteen policemen they were testing ranked low on a masculinity scale built around a series of word associations. Of fifteen occupational categories the police were twelfth, just above editors, clergymen, and artists. The scientists' first reaction was disbelief:

> Are policemen really as feminine mentally as this rating indicates, or have we through unfortunate chance secured scores from an unusual sampling? In order to check the results 15 more policemen, members of the force in a large California city were given the M-F test. Results corroborated the first study.[63]

Six of these additional tests were incomplete and could not be used. The nine valid ones scored low in masculinity like the first group.

Apparently stimulated by these results, Terman and Miles sent questionnaires to forty-two eminent psychologists working in the field of personality study. They were asked to rank twenty male occupations according to masculinity-femininity. Almost without exception the respondents ranked the policemen and firemen as the most masculine of all occupational groups, whereas Terman and Miles had test data placing them at the sixteenth position.

Terman and Miles assume that the personality theorists were misled by superficial appearances, and therefore were

---

See, for example, John Rechy, *City of Night* (New York: Grove Press Inc., 1963), pp. 132–133; Jean Genet, *The Thief's Journal* (New York: Grove Press Inc., 1964), pp. 188–200; and Donald W. Cory and John P. LeRoy, *The Homosexual and His Society* (New York: The Citadel Press, 1963), pp. 132–133.

[62] Lewis M. Terman and Catherine C. Miles, *op. cit.*, p. 164.

[63] *Ibid.*, p. 175, footnote 1.

wrong in their judgment. They do not doubt the validity of their own data, although the total number of policemen in the sample, including the replication, was only twenty-two.

> It appears that the judges failed to make allowances for the masculinizing effect of a male uniform and for specific occupational selection in terms of stature. Also they overlooked two selective factors that have probably entered: (1) the craving of some effeminate men for uniforms as a means of enhancing their feelings of masculinity, and (2) the avoidance of ill-paid and rather routine civil-service jobs by men who have in pronounced degree the masculine qualities of aggressiveness, self-confidence, and independence.[64]

Even so, evidence for homosexual motivations in police behavior remains insignificant. A virile policeman's concern with sexuality connotes no lack of masculinity. His ambivalence toward women results from the occupation's sad experience with the fair sex, and seems at least as much related to practical experience as to unconscious psychological motivations. The same applies to the policeman's overpowering dislike for homosexuals and sex offenders. Reflecting the socially approved attitude popular in society, the policeman will gain greater tolerance for homosexuals, as the public does.

Latent Hypochondria

The most valid of prevalent stereotypes is that of the police appointee as a superb physical specimen. In the Academy recruits are put through a grueling series of exercises: running (several miles each day), boxing, judo. After six months in the precinct these stoic Spartans are transformed. They have become hypochondriacs.

[64] *Ibid.*, p. 456.

Possibly, men with splendid physiques are unnaturally prone to this syndrome. Stories about the denizens of Muscle Beach near Santa Monica, California (so named because weight lifters and body builders congregate there), confirm this. But there are legitimate reasons for this hypochondria: difficult tours of duty, beat-pounding in winter, freezing in front of a fixed post, or directing traffic at a busy school crossing in a blizzard.

Policemen are, in fact, the natural victims of many occupational ailments—arthritis, rheumatism, sinusitis, varicose veins, ulcers, and heart trouble. The Patrolmen's Benevolent Association in New York has fought to pass a bill in the State Legislature that will officially recognize "heart disease as a disability incurred in the line of duty unless specifically proved otherwise."[65] The police magazine, *Spring 3100*, regularly publishes articles on health and bodily care, in a sense officially fostering latent hypochondria.

A large share of the policeman's background is concerned with prosaic subjects: how to keep feet warm in zero weather, the best type of winter underwear, the most comfortable shoes, how to prevent or cure colds, and especially how to prime the heater in the radio car. For a while the rookie scoffs at the thought that he would ever become so effete that he would wear "long johns." The experienced cop nods cynically. He hears this every year during early November when it is still relatively warm. In the middle of January the old-timer cannot help but feel a little spark of triumph when he notices the heavy long underwear gracing or disgracing that brash young "buffalo" who thought he could prevail against the wisdom of the job. This awareness of the body also has positive functions. To prevent bodily

[65] New York's Finest: *The Official PBA Publication*, Vol. 10 (December 1961), p. 3.

deterioration, many policemen become devotees of weight lifting and body building. The added strength is a great asset in handling criminals, carrying stretchers, and looking impressive in uniform. Without this concern the little joys of life would pass unnoticed. Perhaps in this spirit, the old-timer encourages a nervous rookie on a rainy day by repeating one of the hoary old maxims, "A good cop never gets wet."

Specific duties connected with the police role sometimes induce a subdued form of hypochondria. Whenever someone calls an ambulance, a policeman goes to the scene to render aid and obtain the necessary information for police records, thereby quickly becoming an intimate of nurses, interns, and doctors. The hospital becomes his hangout where he is periodically called to complete the police reports required in a great variety of hospital cases. As Goffman puts it, the cop is privileged to enter the backstage region behind the footlights where the social front is dropped.[66] Policemen watch doctors operate, help dress wounds, discuss symptoms. While waiting they often read one of the volumes on diagnostic medicine usually found in the emergency room.

The policeman's normal occupational concern for his health and this smattering of medical information prompt him to try to diagnose his own ills. That burning sensation in the abdomen may herald the duodenal ulcer about which he was reading an hour earlier. The pain in the chest after climbing six flights of stairs signals to this self-educated diagnostician a possible coronary, or at best a case of angina pectoris. It is not surprising that he is a hypochondriac.

In their weaker moments policemen are addicted to an institutionalized mirage, the wish-fulfillment dream of "three-quarters." Policemen seriously incapacitated in the per-

[66] Erving Goffman, *The Presentation of Self in Everyday Life, op. cit.,* pp. 106–140.

formance of duty may be retired long before finishing their twenty years of service, with an annual pension of three-quarters of their yearly salary; and this pension is forever tax exempt! Stories constantly circulate describing in fine detail how certain injured members of the force remained crippled for months while awaiting the final decision on their application for disability retirement at three-quarters pay. When the notification of approval arrives, so the legends go, they throw away the crutches, jump out of bed or the wheelchair, and spend the rest of their lives in the pursuit of quiet enjoyments befitting their invalid state—tennis, skiing, and mountain climbing. Pleasant hours on post are whiled away in imagining what minor injury and ingenious dealings might con the board of examining surgeons into approving a request for three-quarters.[67] Consequently, when a member of the force is seriously incapacitated, and does receive a medical discharge, he is more often envied than pitied.

The Allocation of Authoritarian Patrolmen

Despite the best efforts of the training program police recruits vary in the amount of authoritarianism they absorb. This may be a result of the different impact of training, experience, and role models upon each individual. The system places the most authoritarian men where they have most opportunity to demonstrate authoritarianism.[68] This is a

[67] This hope combined with the typical police cynicism was probably the reason that one veteran policeman reportedly visited a police surgeon and tossed an envelope containing several thousand dollars on his desk in an apparent attempt to bribe the surgeon to approve a medical discharge. See New York *Post*, July 11, 1965, p. 53.

[68] An analogous combination of self-selection and administrative decision placed the most brutal inmates of the German concentration camps in positions where they could exercise police power over the other prisoners. See Viktor E. Frankl, *Man's Search for Meaning, op. cit.*, p. 7.

latent consequence of the normal bureaucratic personnel administration. It is the patrolman on the beat who is involved in most of the incidents that require a display of authority. It is precisely the patrolman on the beat who is most authoritarian.

Once the recruit becomes part of the system, occupational forces tend to transform him into an authoritarian agent of control. To those who find this distasteful and can resist authoritarianism to some extent, a solution is available. Where the motivation is strong enough, they are usually successful in obtaining an assignment which emphasizes service rather than control. They may work in the Youth Division, the Emergency Service Division, or as clerks, typists, and stenographers.

From one point of view the system has failed with the few policemen who are not transformed into authoritarian personalities. But from the insensitive standpoint of the peer group it is not the system, but the deviant nonauthoritarian individual who is the failure. Because he does not inspire enough confidence in his colleagues and his superiors, he often is relegated to the quiet posts or to jobs that do not require active police work.

As *The Authoritarian Personality* studies consistently show, more highly educated persons are lower in authoritarianism. The more highly educated policeman naturally has a far higher rate of success on promotion tests which call for knowledge and writing ability, rather than for meritorious police service. As they are promoted to the higher ranks the less authoritarian, better educated policemen are drawn away from the lower echelons in the street.

As a result of administrative pressures on commanders of patrol precincts, a counterforce accelerates this process. Because there seems to be no other short-range answer to the problem of establishing "law and order" in tough, crime-ridden areas, the policy of superior officers is to assign the toughest cops to these locations. Thus, a high percentage of authoritarian types becomes concentrated in situations permitting unrestrained use of force.

The hostility and fear that almost palpably press against a policeman in lower-class areas, aggravate his impulse to "get tough."

> For the urban poor, the police are those who arrest you. In almost any slum there is a vast conspiracy against the forces of law and order. If someone approaches asking for a person, no one there will have heard of him, even if he lives next door. The outsider is "cop," . . . (and, in the Negro ghetto, most dramatically, he is "the Man").[69]

In summary, there is a social process at work within the police system that precipitates the most authoritarian type into the authoritarian role at the lowest level of the hierarchy, pounding the beat. Only after many years, when he is too old to stand the pace, is he rewarded with a quiet job in the station house as messenger or attendant. There, as an elder statesman, he transmits his reverence for toughness to each new generation of recruits.

The doctrine of the professional movement advocates education, a non-punitive orientation, strict legality in every phase of police work and, most important of all, good public relations. These principles create an atmosphere in which only the professionally directed police officer can operate successfully. On a lower plane within the hierarchy, exists the tough-minded, authoritarian working class of the police society. Conditions at this level foster an outlook that exalts

[69] Michael Harrington, *The Other America* (New York: The Macmillan Co., 1964), p. 16.

power and force, and is contemptuous of the so-called un-realistic, soft-minded, and even subversive ideas of the professionals. Different value systems, ranks, and assignments create the two poles: the most authoritarian policemen work at the bottom of the police occupation in the streets; the most professional generally rise to the higher ranks and the preferred administrative assignments.

Although the two classes are constantly at odds, this internecine struggle must be kept under cover; at all costs a united front must be presented for public inspection. The salary raises and legal concessions both groups desire depend on how well this united image is accepted by the public. The dilemma of the contemporary urban police system is that it must produce both classes and inevitably polarize them. Law enforcement oscillates from one philosophy to the other.

The source of police authoritarianism is a recurrent question. I have taken the position that authoritarianism develops after appointment as a result of socialization and experience in the police social system. The opposing view is that long before appointment, a self-selection process predisposes those who are authoritarians to police work. This latter thesis ascribes police authoritarianism to the personality variable rather than to factors of the social system.

Because there are few definitive related studies[70] and because social scientists have had limited intimate experience in this area, the fundamental source of evidence necessarily depends upon the general sociological and psychological characteristics of the group in question.

[70] Most of the reported research concerns subjects who were already policemen at the time of the study. There have been reports by psychiatrists hired by police departments to screen applicants. But they usually end up by rejecting candidates with unfavorable personality syndromes, and this would include extreme authoritarianism.

Police candidates are male. They are young, ranging from their late teens to the late twenties. They are physically above average, strong, and athletic. The great majority have high school diplomas or the equivalent. Most come from working-class backgrounds. In general, they are white, predominantly Catholic, and to a lesser degree Irish. All know that they have chosen to enter a quasi-military occupation that requires the use of force and lethal weapons. Preliminary investigation of their backgrounds eliminates radicals and applicants with criminal records. Of all the hopeful aspirants only ten to fifteen per cent are eventually appointed. The most popular motivations for choosing the police occupation include security, public service, adventure, family tradition, and the appeal of the uniform and the authority it connotes.

Fortunately, most of these descriptive categories: sex, age, religion, physique, intelligence and education, motivation, and class have been studied in connection with authoritarianism. From the published reports we can make some legitimate deductions about police candidates.

Among the few who might advance the hypothesis that authoritarianism can be completely equated with masculinity is Simone de Beauvoir. She asserts that men are aggressors because they subjugate women by the position assumed in the sexual embrace.[71] If this is so, then every male occupation is by definition authoritarian. It is of some interest that men did score slightly higher than women on the F scale, thereby creating circumstantial evidence that men are more authoritarian; however, researchers advise that the results "may not reflect a true sex difference since they are not based on comparable groups of men and women."[72] Even if men are more authoritarian than women, this fact does not

[71] Simone de Beauvoir, The Second Sex (Alfred A. Knopf, 1953).
[72] T. W. Adorno, et al., op. cit., p. 138.

justify any assumption about the range of authoritarianism among men.

Age is another factor that correlates positively with authoritarianism. In a careful replication study of authoritarianism, Morris Janowitz and Dwaine Marvick found that, "First there was a statistically significant tendency for younger people to register as 'low authoritarians' more frequently than did older people."[73] Therefore, the youth of the neophyte policemen would reduce the probability of high authoritarianism.

Religion may have some bearing on the case especially because Catholics are heavily represented on the major urban police forces, but there is conflicting evidence on this point. Adorno and his colleagues found that "The factor of religious denomination does not prove to be very significant. Among the largest denominations no differences of any significance appear."[74] In a study by Daniel J. Levinson and Phyllis E. Huffman Catholics were found to be more authoritarian than other religious groups, but showed great variation among themselves.[75]

The stereotype of the policeman with the Irish brogue happens to be based on fact. Irishmen are strongly attracted to the police force. Cultural tradition almost requires one son of an Irish American working-class family to be a policeman, another a priest, jobs that have, as described above, striking parallels. The police force has been called "the classic stronghold" of the Irish.[76] Former New York City Police Com-

---

[73] Morris Janowitz and Dwaine Marvick, "Authoritarianism and Political Behavior," *Public Opinion Quarterly*, Vol. 17 (Summer 1953), p. 191.

[74] Adorno, *et al.*, *op. cit.*, p. 220.

[75] Daniel J. Levinson and Phyllis E. Huffman, "Traditional Family Ideology and Its Relation to Personality," *Journal of Personality*, Vol. 23 (1955), p. 265. Rokeach cites studies of a similar import. See Milton Rokeach, *The Open and Closed Mind* (New York: Basic Books, Inc., 1960), pp. 110–119.

[76] Nathan Glazer and Daniel P. Moynihan, *op. cit.*, p. 261.

missioner Francis Adams remarked, half seriously, that "If it weren't for the Irish, there would be no police. And if it weren't for the Irish, there would be no need for them."[77]

It is very difficult to obtain exact figures on the racial, ethnic, or religious composition of a large police force. However, it is possible to make an educated guess in the case of the New York City Police Department. *Spring 3100* publishes membership figures of officially recognized organizations. The major religious and ethnic groups have their own social and fraternal associations whose members have joined them for various reasons. Each organization usually includes a small percentage of retired policemen. For this reason the figures give only an approximation, but withal a fairly reliable basis for comparison, as shown in Table VI.

TABLE VI
COMPARISON OF MEMBERSHIP OF SELECTED POLICE SOCIETIES[78]

Name of Association	Background of Membership	Number of Members	Per Cent
Emerald Society	Irish	8,500	42 %
Columbia Association	Italian	5,000	25
Shomrim Society	Jewish	2,270	11.2
Steuben Association	German	1,500	7.4
Guardians Association	Negro	1,320	6.5
Pulaski Association	Polish	1,100	5.4
St. Paul Society	Greek and Russian	300	1.5
Hispanic Society	Puerto Rican and Spanish	250	1
	Total	20,240	100 %

It was estimated that approximately eleven thousand members of the force (forty per cent) are Irish.[79] In comparison

[77] Statement made by former Commissioner Francis Adams on TV program entitled *Crime and the Cities*, May 17, 1964.

[78] SOURCE: *Spring 3100*, Vol. 36 (March 1965), pp. 21–26.

[79] Personal conversation with high officials and delegates of the Emerald Society.

the Irish ethnic group numbers only ten per cent of the total New York City population.[80]

Until someone proves conclusively that the Irish are more authoritarian than other ethnic groups, the predominance of Irish in the police force does not resolve the problem of police authoritarianism. There is no reason to suppose that Irishmen join the force for any motive other than security, as do the other applicants. The author of a popular book describing American-Irish life and customs agrees that the reason "why so many Irish have joined the police force, down through the years, is that lacking capital, often the victims of prejudice, they sought security."[81]

There may be some question about a police candidate modal personality; there can be none about the basic physique of the candidate group. It falls perfectly into the mesomorph classification assigned to this somatotype by William H. Sheldon, the controversial constitutional psychologist. According to Sheldon, mesomorphy is highly correlated (.82) with the temperament he has designated as Somatotonia.[82] This temperament is characterized by assertiveness, dominance, lust for power, competitive aggressiveness, ruthlessness, and several other qualities associated with authoritarianism.[83]

---

[80] Glazer and Moynihan, op. cit., p. 19.

[81] Bob Considine, It's the Irish (Garden City: Doubleday & Co., 1961), pp. 110–111. On the other hand James Wilson suggests that some Irish candidates join the force because they have better chances of being promoted. However, this would not apply to the New York police force because promotion at least through captain depends on civil service examinations. See James Q. Wilson, "Generational and Ethnic Differences among Career Police Officers," American Journal of Sociology, Vol. 69 (March 1964), pp. 522–528.

[82] William H. Sheldon, The Varieties of Temperament: A Psychology of Constitutional Differences (New York: Harper, 1942), p. 400.

[83] Ibid., p. 26.

After police applicants have undergone the competitive physical test, there is a still higher percentage of mesomorphs. The endomorphs (fat) are ordinarily too slow to run the mile or complete the agility obstacle course in the required time. The ectomorphs (thin) are rarely strong enough to compete with the mesomorphs in weight lifting. Therefore, Sheldon's somatotype theory may partially account for authoritarian personalities among police candidates.

To balance the equation it should be noted that Geoffrey Gorer, the anthropologist who has devoted his major effort to the concept of modal personality, suggests that in England the "superior" physique of the policeman may have the opposite effect and thus be correlated with a reduction of authoritarian traits.

> This means that most of the police recruits come from a small and (statistically speaking) physically unrepresentative section of the population, perhaps some 10 per cent of the whole; and, although the connection between physique and character is still comparatively undetermined, the folk observation that big men are likely to be easy-going, even tempered, just, and slow to anger may well have some foundation in fact. Although the minimum height was probably imposed with the intention of securing physically strong and impressive men, it may well have had the secondary effect of securing that recruits were selected from people of constitutionally equable temperament.[84]

While Sheldon's work has many virtues, some critics have expressed at least doubt of its validity.[85] Certainly the work

[84] Geoffrey Gorer, "Modification of National Character: The Role of the Police in England," in *Personal Character and Cultural Milieu*, ed. Douglas G. Haring (Syracuse: Syracuse University Press, 1956), p. 333.
[85] See for example: Calvin S. Hall and Gardner Lindzey, *Theories of Personality* (New York: John Wiley and Sons, 1957), pp. 371–374; David G. McClelland, *Personality* (New York: The Dryden Press, 1955), pp. 127–130; H. J. Eysenck, *The Structure of Human Personality* (New York:

contains methodological flaws because the author himself set up the variables and performed the interviews and measurements. The correlations, therefore, tend to reflect his preconceptions rather than objective facts. Moreover, the three somatotypes and the corresponding temperaments are not so clear and invariant as Sheldon would have the reader believe. The varieties of temperament, when factor-analyzed by others, yield two, not three types.[86] Finally, it is alleged, obvious errors in computation mar the accuracy of the conclusions.[87] According to two outstanding personality theorists, who independently reached similar negative evaluations of Sheldon's typology,

> One of the weaknesses of psychologists has been that whenever they develop a new measuring instrument they tend to try to generalize it to cover the whole of personality. We shall meet this tendency again and again in subsequent discussions of other approaches to personality. The term somatotonia is at once too broad and too narrow. It is too broad in including areas of personality which may be better conceptualized in other terms, and it is too narrow in assuming that wide areas of personality can best be described in physique-related terms.[88]

In general, we may sum up Sheldon's contribution by emphasizing the novelty and comprehensiveness of his approach, the persistence of his endeavours, and the quantitative form

---

John Wiley and Sons, 1953), pp. 69–72; C. J. Adcock, "A Factorial Examination of Sheldon's Types," *Journal of Personality*, Vol. 16 (1948), pp. 312–319; A. Lubin, "A Note on Sheldon's Table of Correlations Between Temperamental Traits," *British Journal of Psychology, Statistical Section*, Vol. 3 (1950), pp. 186–189; Lloyd G. Humphries, "Characteristics of Type Concepts with Special Reference to Sheldon's Typology," *Psychological Bulletin*, Vol. 54 (1957), pp. 218–228.

[86] Eysenck, *op. cit.*, pp. 69–70.

[87] *Ibid.*, pp. 69, 72.

[88] McClelland, *op. cit.*, p. 129.

in which his estimates are given. What militates against acceptance of his scheme is the extremely subjective character of the ratings, the obvious statistical errors in his computations, and the failure to use appropriate methods of analysis for the correlations he reports.[89]

The third analyst delivers the *coup de grace:*

> Sheldon's claim for having established relationships between physique and temperament are thus "thrown out of court" for lack of evidence. More basic, however, is the doubt cast on the validity of his type concepts. His temperament types were arbitrarily determined by the statistical criteria. His physical types arose from the armchair.[90]

Although Sheldon does not fare too well with his psychologist colleagues, sociologists are even more resistant to his findings. They continue to maintain that the best way to understand personality within social systems is to study it in connection with role behavior. Physique is only one of many variables of undetermined significance that must all be considered. As with several other descriptive items, it is too early to conclude that the modal mesomorph physique of police candidates indicates their authoritarian orientation.

The next variables to be examined are intelligence and education. The educational background of police candidates offers no real clue either. Graduation from high school is not remarkable one way or the other, nor is the fact that most members of the group invariably have an I.Q. of 100 to 105. From all that is known about the selection process, we may assume that the most educated and most intelligent police candidates will survive the various hurdles with greater frequency than those with less education and intelligence, i.e., those who have the qualities associated with a lower

[89] Eysenck, *op. cit.*, p. 72.
[90] Humphries, *op. cit.*, p. 222.

degree of authoritarianism[91] are more likely to be chosen.

In the preliminary character and background investigation, applicants who reveal extreme deviance are eliminated. Among authoritarian individuals certain syndromes often occur that preclude the appointment of such types as the rebel, the tough guy, the hoodlum, the asocial, the fascist, the crank, and the psychopath.[92] A report covering the period 1953–1956 indicated that eleven per cent of the applicants for the Los Angeles Police Department were rejected because they did not meet acceptable psychiatric standards. Some of those rejects failed because they were aggressive personalities.[93] However, it should not be assumed that those remaining are highly submissive to authority—a trait that is connected with authoritarian personality.

If it could be shown that men are drawn into the police force through a desire to arrest criminals, demonstrate power, fight crime, regulate or prevent public action, or lured by the potential adventure and glamour of police work we might conclude that police work mainly attracted authoritarians. But the fact that security is the most frequent reason for the choice invalidates this assumption. Eli Ginzberg and his colleagues maintain that there is a definite relation between occupational choice and personality needs.[94] It is instructive to note that they report an interview with a working-class teen-ager who intended to become a policeman. As his responses indicate, security, first, then service, determined his choice.

[91] Richard Christie and Marie Jahoda, eds., *Studies in the Scope and Method of the Authoritarian Personality* (Glencoe: The Free Press, 1954), pp. 167–172.

[92] T. W. Adorno, *et al., op. cit.*, pp. 762–767.

[93] James H. Rankin, "Preventive Psychiatry in the Los Angeles Police Department," *op. cit.*, p. 4.

[94] Eli Ginzberg, *et al., op. cit.*

Q. What are the advantages of being on the police force?

A. You serve twenty years and then get a pension; you carry hospitalization for the family.[95]

Q. If you had no need to make money, what would you consider an ideal job?

A. Still the police force.

Q. What do you like about it?

A. Just the idea to help somebody in some way or another. You're always bound to help somebody. I've talked to cops.[96]

In a series of studies conducted at the New York Police Academy from 1957 to 1961, security was the principal motivation that emerged in at least sixty per cent of the cases. Robert Bird in 1960 wrote an interesting series of articles on the New York City Police Department, which appeared in the New York *Herald Tribune* under the title, "Cops or Social Scientists?" He questioned such experts as Stephen P. Kennedy, then Police Commissioner, Deputy Police Commissioner Alexander Aldrich, and other leading officials about this very subject and received similar replies.

> Police officials say that when these men are asked why they want to join the police force, the overwhelming majority answer because of security. When asked what they mean by security, they explain, freedom from lay-offs.[97]

Dr. James Rankin, who has interviewed and tested thousands of candidates for the Los Angeles Police Department, concludes that "A high percentage of applicants for police jobs are attracted by 'security' advantages."[98] And from the Midwest there is another echo.

[95] *Ibid.*, p. 156.
[96] *Ibid.*, p. 157.
[97] Robert S. Bird, "Cops or Social Scientists?", New York *Herald Tribune*, July 17, 1960, p. 16.
[98] Rankin, "Preventive Psychiatry in the Los Angeles Police Department," *op. cit.*, p. 6.

> The preceding material suggests that men who decide to join the police department are drawn from large, working-class families . . . and emphasize security as a major reason for joining the department.[99]

Security, particularly economic security, may well be the motivation for joining. But what about the cognitive component? Police candidates know that their duties require the use of lethal weapons, and that force and violence are the stock in trade of the successful patrolman. Does not this indicate that they are incipient authoritarians? Contact with thousands of recruits shows that most new recruits accept the revolver and the nightstick with a neutral attitude which they display from the first day of service and which, we may suppose, reflects and continues their feelings before appointment. Moreover, when the candidates learn the terrible responsibility of safeguarding the gun, this symbol of authority loses whatever glamour it may have possessed. It would thus seem unwarranted to conclude that accepting the responsibility and necessity for authority and force demonstrates an eagerness to use them. It is more tenable to maintain that force is a necessary evil which is one of the more unattractive aspects of the police job.

The last variable related to authoritarianism is the working-class background of police candidates. As we have come to expect, there is no clear-cut agreement about the quality or direction of the relation. The politics of the radical left apotheosize the working class and condemn the police. The proletariat, it is maintained, embody the force that eventually will create a social Utopia. This belief is to a certain extent mirrored in the writings of many philosophers who blame

[99] Westley, "The Police: A Sociological Study of Law, Custom, and Morality," *op. cit.*, p. 83.

the anxiety of our time on the alienation of the worker from his product, and who would reinstate the era of the craftsman. Nostalgically they imply that the worker would thus recover his original state of contentment and virtue. However, this myth of the nobility of the proletariat was shattered by clear evidence that in many countries the working class has been only too ready to espouse the cause of totalitarian movements.

Gradually, the pendulum has swung in the other direction until now there is strong support for the theory of working-class authoritarianism. *The Authoritarian Personality* hints of this new trend. Of the fourteen groups who completed the F scale, San Quentin prisoners scored highest in authoritarianism; working-class men next highest. Most of the San Quentin group came from the working class. This high degree of working-class authoritarianism

> will come as a surprise only to those who have become accustomed to explaining all important differences in social attitudes on the basis of socio-economic group membership, and who look to the working man as the main carrier of liberal ideas. It is true, of course, as a matter of economic and social fact, that the crucial role in the struggle against increasing concentration of economic power will have to be played by the working people, acting in accordance with their self-interest, but it is foolhardy to underestimate the susceptibility to fascist propaganda within these masses themselves. For our part, we see no reason to suppose that the authoritarian structures with which we are concerned would be any less well developed in the working class than in other segments of the population.[100]

Seymour M. Lipset has become an outstanding spokesman and defender of the position that authoritarianism is prevalent

[100] T. W. Adorno, *et al.*, *op. cit.*, p. 267.

among the lower class. He has collected data from the major nations of the world that lend credence to his conclusion that "the lower strata are the least tolerant."[101] In addition, many studies that he summarized, "show a consistent association between authoritarianism and lower-class status."[102] According to Lipset, working-class authoritarianism arises from the typical conditions of lower-class life.

> A number of elements contribute to authoritarian predispositions in lower-class individuals. Low education, low participation in political or voluntary organizations of any type, little reading, isolated occupations, economic insecurity, and authoritarian family patterns are some of the most important. These elements are interrelated, but they are by no means identical.[103]

Corroboration of Lipset's theory appears in an excellent critique of *The Authoritarian Personality* studies in which Christie adduces further evidence on the same subject.

> Anyone familiar with lower socio-economic groupings can scarcely be unaware of the fact that there is realistic justification for their view that the world is indeed junglelike and capricious. They have no relatives or friends with the power to intercede successfully when they are rightly or wrongly accused of legal offenses. Even relatively minor figures in the hierarchy of power are identified with omnipotent forces—police officers are referred to as "The Law" . . .[104]

> It is a tenable hypothesis that a basic reason for the greater acceptance of F scale items among members of lower socioeconomic groupings as contrasted with middle-class individuals is related to the reality of the referent in the items.[105]

---

[101] Seymour M. Lipset, *Political Man* (Garden City: Doubleday & Co., Inc., 1963), p. 94.
[102] *Ibid.*, p. 96.
[103] *Ibid.*, pp. 100–101.
[104] Christie and Jahoda, *op. cit.*, p. 175.
[105] *Ibid.*

Lipset's thesis is controversial enough to have stimulated other social scientists to analyze this new breed of proletarian. S. M. Miller and Frank Riessman[106] have proposed several criticisms of "working-class authoritarianism" that justify the withholding of judgment on what seemed before an established fact. They have done this without recourse to the starry-eyed view of the workingman as the source of all that is noble in society.

Accordingly, they call attention to several questionable assumptions that affect the validity of Lipset's conclusions. In the first place, the standard or yardstick of democracy that Lipset employed is not widely accepted, therefore, the fact that working-class members do not particularly worship democracy's ideological planks should not be interpreted as implicit receptivity to authoritarian forces. In this connection an instructive parallel can be found in the critique by Edward A. Shils of the concept of democracy utilized in *The Authoritarian Personality*. The items that were expected to be answered positively by democratic personalities

> are most often the commonplaces of the "left" intelligentsia—of those who approved the New Deal and more particularly those who in the late 40's sympathized with Mr. Henry Wallace and the Progressive Party.[107]

"This narrowness of political imagination, this holding fast to a deforming intellectual tradition,"[108] in Shils' opinion, is a significant deficiency in *The Authoritarian Personality*. This is exactly the criticism that Miller and Riessman lodge against Lipset.

[106] S. M. Miller and Frank Riessman, "Working Class Authoritarianism: A Critique of Lipset," *British Journal of Sociology*, Vol. 12 (1961), pp. 263–276.

[107] Edward A. Shils, "Authoritarianism: 'Right' and 'Left,'" in Christie and Jahoda, *op. cit.*, p. 29.

[108] *Ibid.*, p. 31.

A second damaging challenge questions the validity and reliability of the F scale. Miller and Riessman doubt that the content of the F scale and the responses to it have the same general import for the working class as they do for the middle class to whom the test was primarily directed.[109] The traditionalism of the lower class is easily confused with the middle-class conventionalism envisaged by the creators of the F scale. Similarly, a strong desire for structure and stability, a realistic response to the vicissitudes of existence in the working-class subculture, may be wrongly equated with submission to authority, which in the F scale denotes an entirely different pattern.

Miller and Riessman are also skeptical about the ultimate purpose of the F scale. Since it was originally intended to measure personality, is it legitimate to assume that it measures attitudes just as well? After a review of the copious literature the two critics reach the following conclusions:

> There is growing evidence that present-day authoritarianism scales as well as many other instruments are not validly used on working-class groups.[110]

> Neither class, we believe, is psychologically authoritarian, but both classes have values which could be turned in the direction of political authoritarianism under certain conditions.[111]

The working class constitutes from forty to fifty per cent of our population.[112] If the F scale is a valid index of authoritarianism for any class and the average score of the

---

[109] Miller and Riessman, *op. cit.*, p. 264.

[110] *Ibid.*, p. 272.

[111] *Ibid.*

[112] Richard Centers, *Psychology of Social Classes* (Princeton: Princeton University Press, 1949), pp. 76–77; Joseph A. Kahl, *The American Class Structure* (New York: Rinehart, 1957), p. 187.

working class is higher than that of the middle class, it follows that at least one-half of the working class must be below the mean in authoritarianism, and at least several million of the working class very low in authoritarianism. The mere fact that many police applicants come from the working class indicates nothing about their degree of authoritarianism; without proof that self-selection of personality types operates they may come from the part of the working class that is low in authoritarianism, as Gorer assumes in his description of the English policeman.

How does the working-class youth choose a career in law enforcement? Let us consider the dilemma of a high-school graduate without special talent or training. Good positions are often denied newcomers because of union rules or seniority provisions, even when no special ability is required, and rarely do salaries for non-specialized work go beyond seventy-five dollars a week.

Frustrated elsewhere, our job seeker turns to civil service where there is good pay, security, and decent working conditions. For which positions can he qualify? The obvious choices are jobs in the post office, sanitation, fire, and police departments. His high-school diploma is enough to satisfy entrance conditions. In each case there is a competitive test of roughly equivalent difficulty. But the post office position is federal, and does not pay as well, nor does it have the same early retirement policy as a city job. A sanitation worker does not enjoy as high a status as a fireman or a policeman. A fireman must live indoors with a small group of men and constantly be exposed to fire and smoke. On the other hand, the police position pays very well and offers among its advantages a life outdoors with possibilities of romance and adventure. The police job is an obvious choice for a young man of lower-class background. It matters little what type of personality he possesses.

One remaining confusion must be eliminated. The expression "working-class background" is often employed as a loose synonym for lower class, but it seems that are two lower classes. The lower lower class as described by Albert K. Cohen and Harold M. Hodges is characterized by anti-intellectuality, authoritarianism, pessimism-insecurity, and misanthropy.[113] Most reports agree that the lower lower class tends to have irregular work habits with long periods of unemployment, and that its members are chronic offenders. In fact, in the study of Yankee City, W. Lloyd Warner found that one in every three persons in the lower lower class had been arrested.[114]

The upper segment of the lower class is euphemistically called the working class. Cohen and Hodges constantly assert that people on this level differed significantly from those beneath them on the social scale. In many important respects the working class was indistinguishable from the law-abiding lower middle class.[115]

Police candidates by and large come from the working class. The strict police investigation eliminates many applicants from the lower lower class because of unemployment and arrest records.[116] Secondly, the educational requirement

[113] Albert K. Cohen and Harold M. Hodges, "Characteristics of the Lower-Blue-Color-Class," *Social Problems*, Vol. 10 (Spring 1963), pp. 303–334.

[114] See W. Lloyd Warner, *Yankee City* (New Haven: Yale University Press, 1963), pp. 262–265; W. Lloyd Warner, *Social Class in America* (New York: Harper and Row, 1960); August B. Hollingshead, *Elmtown's Youth* (New York: John Wiley and Sons, Inc., 1963); Joseph Kahl, *The American Class Structure, op. cit.;* Bennett M. Berger, *Working Class Suburb* (Berkeley and Los Angeles: The University of California Press, 1960).

[115] Cohen and Hodges, *op. cit.*, pp. 312, 315, 332, 333.

[116] There is one loophole through which police candidates with poor records may obtain entrance to the New York City Police Department. It

of a high-school or equivalency diploma prevents the admission of many in this lower group.

Finally, the clinching argument against a modal class personality attacks the concept of class itself. As Miller says, any generalization that views a class as a homogeneous body is suspect because a class is composed of innumerable, disparate elements; therefore, the concept of class, established as a basis for generalizations, is itself of questionable validity.[117]

Nevertheless, whatever its shortcomings the F scale is still a principal instrument to measure personality,[118] and, as such, necessary to a study of police authoritarianism. Very generously John McNamara, director of a research project concerned with the selection and training of members of the New York City Police Department, agreed to administer a

---

is the "one in three rule" that grants the right, but also the obligation, to the Commissioner to choose at least one of each three consecutive names on the civil service list, and discretion to pass over the other two. This provides some flexibility of choice. For desirable candidates the rule is never invoked, and all are appointed as a matter of course. But toward the termination of a long list, it sometimes happens that a point is reached when all of the remaining names on the list belong to candidates who have already been passed over once before. Now the rule operates to force the admission of one of each three, whether the Commissioner likes it or not, so long as the objections to his appointment do not bar his appointment by force of law. The total number of policemen admitted under these circumstances is very small—no more than two hundred and fifty, or one per cent of the force. I have discussed this problem with superior officers in the department who had made studies of this subject. In one case I was informed that the records of men in this category were equal to those of the average members of the force. In the second instance it was reported that they had inferior records. In any event their number is so small that the impact of these cases on the police organization is infinitesimal.

[117] S. M. Miller, "The American Lower Class: A Typological Approach," *Social Research*, Vol. 31 (Spring 1964), pp. 21, 22.

[118] Another possible weakness in the F scale is the tendency of people to answer its questions in the same way; this "yeasaying" is also known as the halo effect. For a full discussion of this point see Roger Brown, *Social Psychology* (New York: The Free Press, 1965), pp. 477–546. In that same chapter Brown shows that this response set accounts for only fourteen per cent of the variance and he states unequivocally that "The best measure of authoritarianism is the F scale" (p. 526).

slightly shortened F scale test combined with the Srole
Anomia Scale to 166 police candidates.[119]

Recruited at three different times, residents of many different cities, and almost all from working-class backgrounds,
the candidates had passed the mental, physical, and medical
examinations, and were being investigated prior to appointment.

The group's mean score on the F scale was 4.15,[120] compared to the 4.19 score of the working-class sample in *The
Authoritarian Personality*.[121] The score by extrapolation indicates that police candidates in general are no higher in
authoritarianism than the rest of the working class and also
suggests that there is no self-selection among authoritarian
personalities prior to appointment.

Although Dorothy L. Meier and Wendell Bell found the
working class high in anomia,[122] members of this police candidate group scored low on the Srole Anomia Scale. Under
the instructions given in the test, the possible range of scores
on each of five questions was one to seven; the mean score
for the police candidate group was 2.1. The reason this police candidate group proved less anomic than the average
working-class individual may depend on the absence of forces
that usually create anomia in the whole class. According to
Meier and Bell, the typical lower-class person

[119] Anomia refers to the psychological reaction in individuals similar to,
but distinguishable from *anomie*, which is located in the social structure.
Srole built his scale around five statements with which the respondent
agrees or disagrees. In general they are pessimistic in tone, indicating that
things are getting worse and that there is little that the average man can
do to make them better.

[120] John McNamara (New York: June 1962).

[121] T. W. Adorno, *et al., op. cit.,* pp. 266–267. The scoring system runs
from one to seven. The midpoint is four and is theoretically the neutral
zone. Therefore 4.15 and even 4.19 are about the lowest possible scores
that can still denote an authoritarian personality.

[122] Dorothy L. Meier and Wendell Bell, "Anomia and Achievement of
Life Goals," *American Sociological Review*, Vol. 24 (April 1959), pp. 189–
202. Their thesis is that working-class members are high in anomia.

> [perceives] himself as being at the bottom of the class
> hierarchy and thus lacking the advantages, qualifications,
> and opportunities for achievement, [and] regards his chances
> for the attainment of his life goals—especially those having to
> do with monetary success, power, and prestige—as being
> very slight.[123]

About to move into an occupation that would lift them into
the middle class, the police candidates are near escaping lower
class despair and frustration. Eager and optimistic, they have
no reason to feel anomic at this turning point in their lives.

It seems to me that the above data and conclusions support
the notion that police authoritarianism does not come into the
force along with the recruits, but rather is inculcated in the
men through strenuous socialization. The police occupational system is geared to manufacture the "take charge guy,"
and it succeeds in doing so with outstanding efficiency. It is
the police system, not the personality of the candidate, that is
the more powerful determinant of behavior and ideology.

[123] *Ibid.*, p. 194.

CHAPTER 6

The Police and the Supreme Court

In their official policy statements police administrators oppose third-degree methods. Unofficially, a time-honored occupational ideology, with which probably half the force agrees, excuses the use of force to make suspects "talk." According to this social myth the legal system affords too much protection to evildoers and hamstrings the forces of law and order. Therefore, the police must overcome this handicap with the only measures available to them.

The police want to win both ways. Offensively, they proclaim that with legal cooperation, they could handle the burgeoning crime wave. Defensively, they try to avoid responsibility by pointing out that crime is, after all, a social problem whose complexities are beyond their control.[1] Yale Kamisar, professor of law at the University of Michigan, explains why the police hold these contradictory views.

> The police fear—and not without cause—that the public will blame them for the increase in crime. . . .
>
> But no police force can "put a stop to it." The men on the "firing line" do not greatly affect the crime rate—nor do the courts.[2]

[1] The annual *FBI Uniform Crime Reports* contain an introductory disclaimer in which it is acknowledged that crime is a social problem and that "the law enforcement effort is limited to factors within its control." See *FBI Uniform Crime Reports*—1963, 1964, and 1965.

[2] Yale Kamisar, "Criminals, Cops and the Constitution," *The Nation*, Vol. 199 (November 9, 1964), p. 322.

Kamisar also notes that David Acheson, prosecutor of Washington, D.C., does not think that the police could reduce crime if the Supreme Court gave them more leeway. Acheson has said that

> Changes in court decisions and prosecution procedures would have about the same effect on the crime rate as an aspirin would have on a tumor of the brain.[3]

Even sociologists, generally liberal reformers, cannot agree to condemn the police use of force. One sociologist overstates the police handicap by concluding that the "police have no legal ways in which they can question suspects, so naturally they use illegal ones."[4] Prominent criminologists such as the late Edwin H. Sutherland and Donald R. Cressey adopt a similar point of view.

> The American policeman is in a difficult position, for in order to do his work efficiently he must adopt more power than the law and the formal organization of his department permit. He is responsible for the enforcement of the criminal law and for the maintenance of order, yet he cannot meet these responsibilities under the power and authority granted him.[5]

> Among students of the subject there is almost unanimous agreement that the criminal law and criminal procedure are inadequate for the purpose of controlling crime and administering justice.[6]

The above argument fallaciously assumes that the police use of illegal methods necessarily results from legal restrictions

[3] *Ibid.*, p. 323.

[4] C. Ray Jeffery, "The Sociology of the Police," in *Sociology of Crime*, ed. Joseph S. Roucek (New York: Philosophical Library, 1961), p. 342. And this was before the Mapp, Escobedo, and Miranda decisions, when police were given practically a free hand in their interrogation of suspects.

[5] Edwin H. Sutherland and Donald R. Cressey, *Principles of Criminology* (6th Ed.; New York: J. B. Lippincott Co., 1960), p. 331.

[6] *Ibid.*, pp. 334–335.

on their power. Westley has demonstrated that police brutality depends on a value system that, for extra-legal reasons, and not the difficulty of obtaining evidence, condones the rough treatment of cop-fighters and sexual criminals.[7]

There is no evidence that cop-fighters or sexual criminals, and not other offenders, require excessive force at any time during which they are in custody and the police are preparing the prosecution. It is true that for many sexual crimes some corroboration is necessary to convict the defendant. But this evidence may be of any nature, not necessarily a confession by the prisoner.

Until 1964 there were available to the police many legitimate methods of interrogating suspects before and after arrest, and many scientific instruments such as lie detectors, drunkometers, computers, and special equipment for chemical and physical tests, to supplement the questioner's efforts. What often stymied the policeman was the suspect's right to remain silent. The rich suspect with a lawyer usually did so; it was the poor man without counsel who talked or was made to talk. In 1964 this traditional privilege of the well-to-do was extended to the indigent. The Escobedo case established the right to counsel when a man became a suspect in a police investigation. In 1966 the Supreme Court in *Miranda v. Arizona* clarified a moot point, holding that the police were obligated to inform all persons in custody of their right to remain silent, and their right to assistance of counsel, which would be provided without charge to indigent prisoners.

Sutherland and Cressey state above that students of the

---

[7] William A. Westley, "Violence and the Police," *American Journal of Sociology*, Vol. 59 (July 1953), pp. 34–41. The traditional hatred of cop-fighters and sexual offenders is found today in the New York force. Table V indicates that the police respondents chose cop-fighters and homosexuals as the most disliked groups among the police clientele.

subject almost unanimously find criminal law and procedure inadequate to control crime. I would contend, on the contrary, that there is vast disagreement on the efficacy of the law, judging by reports from newspapers, courts, law schools, and law-enforcement agencies. Naturally, thousands of prisoners believe the law to be fearfully adequate. Every major prison has had to establish at least a rudimentary law library to satisfy the demands of inmates who want to find some flaw in criminal law and procedure that will win them a new trial. Victims of police prejudice and brutality, as well as the civil rights experts who seek justice for them, form another group dissatisfied with the criminal law because it gives the police too much, not too little, power. Judges, lawyers, and political scientists constitute another set of students who do not unanimously agree that law enforcement is severely hampered by the law.

Although this dispute has been seething for decades, a series of Supreme Court decisions in favor of convicted defendants and against the police and the prosecutors have brought the question to a head. A brief synopsis of some significant cases will clarify the points at issue.

Mallory v. United States, 354 U.S. 449 (1957)

In Washington, D.C., Mallory, a nineteen-year-old youth of limited intelligence, was arrested on a charge of rape, detained at police headquarters but not arraigned although several magistrates in session could have heard the case. After hours of fruitless interrogation the police asked the defendant to submit to a lie detector test. They did not tell him of his rights to remain silent, to have the assistance of counsel, and to appear before a magistrate, but examined him with the lie detector for an hour and a half before obtaining a confession. Only then did they arraign him. The Supreme Court reversed his conviction by the lower court principally because of the delay in arraigning the prisoner. The court strictly limited the time for interrogating prisoners, reasoning as follows:

> We cannot sanction this extended delay, resulting in confession, without subordinating the general rule of prompt arraignment to the discretion of arresting officers in finding exceptional circumstances for its disregard. In every case where the police resort to interrogation of an arrested person and secure a confession, they may well claim, and quite sincerely, that they were merely trying to check on the information given by him.
>
> Presumably, whenever the police arrest they must arrest on "probable cause." It is not the function of the police to arrest, as it were, at large and to use an interrogating process at police headquarters in order to determine whom they should charge before a committing magistrate on "probable cause."

The Mallory case was combined with an earlier decision from *McNabb v. United States*, 318 U.S. 332 (1943), to establish the well-known McNabb-Mallory rule that requires the police to arraign a prisoner in federal courts without unnecessary delay. Although this decision was not binding on state courts, it did cause consternation among local police jurisdictions because it threatened to eliminate a traditional police *modus operandi* for solving cases—extended interrogation of suspects prior to arraignment.

Spano v. New York, 360 U.S. 315 (1959)

Spano was indicted for shooting and killing a man who had previously assaulted him in a barroom brawl. He surrendered to the district attorney and, upon the advice of his attorney, who left him in the custody of several law-enforcement officers, refused to answer any questions. Six officers questioned him from 7:15 P.M. until after midnight when he was transferred to a police station house where the interrogation continued.

A probationary patrolman, Bruno, who knew Spano, entreated him to talk, pretending that this was the only way to save Bruno's job. Finally, the prisoner confessed and was convicted and sentenced to death in the state courts.

The Supreme Court reversed the conviction, holding that although no physical force was employed, the confession was, nevertheless involuntary. This decision affirms the principle that police may not use psychological pressure and fatigue to gain a confession from a prisoner.

Mapp v. Ohio, 367 U.S. 643 (1961)

The police heard that Dollree Mapp was concealing in her home a large amount of gambling paraphernalia and a person wanted in connection with a bombing. Miss Mapp refused to admit the police officers without a search warrant. About three hours later the police returned and forcibly broke into the house. When she demanded to see the warrant, one of the officers waved a paper in her face which Miss Mapp grabbed and placed in her bosom. A struggle ensued during which the officer recovered the paper and handcuffed the appellant presumably because she had been belligerent. After forcing her upstairs to the bedroom, the officers searched the house thoroughly. In the basement they found some obscene material, for possession of which the appellant was convicted in the Ohio courts.

The Supreme Court reversed the conviction and established for state as well as federal courts the doctrine that illegally seized materials could not be admitted as evidence. Up to this point state courts had not excluded evidence illegally seized by state or city policemen. On the question of whether or not this decision would impair the quality and efficiency of law enforcement, the Supreme Court cited approvingly this excerpt from *Miller v. United States*, 357 U.S. 301 (1957).

> However much in a particular case insistence upon such rules may appear as a technicality that inures to the benefit of a guilty person, the history of the criminal law proves that tolerance of shortcut methods in law enforcement impairs its enduring effectiveness.

The court also pointed to the FBI that from its inception has operated on this principle.

> Yet it has not been suggested either that the Federal Bureau of Investigation has thereby been rendered ineffective, or that the administration of criminal justice in the federal courts has thereby been disrupted.

Escobedo v. Illinois, 378 U.S. 478 (1964)

Escobedo is an extension of the famous case of *Gideon v. Wainwright*, 372 U.S. 335 (1963), in which the court held that every defendant in a felony case has the right to be represented by counsel in court even though he cannot pay the fees. Escobedo was being questioned at the station house in connection with a murder. The police did not inform him of his right to remain silent, and they would not allow him to speak with his attorney, who was at the station house.

A policeman friend of the prisoner urged him to talk, promising that he could go home afterward. On the basis of his revelations Escobedo was indicted for the killing and convicted.

The Supreme Court reversed the conviction and extended the Gideon doctrine from the court to the station house, holding that even during the preliminary investigation

> when the process shifts from investigatory to accusatory—when its focus is on the accused and its purpose is to elicit a confession—our adversary system begins to operate, and, under the circumstances here, the accused must be permitted to consult with his lawyer.

These last two cases, Mapp and Escobedo, have become *causes célèbres*. The Mapp case produced a frantic torrent of complaints from outraged police who felt they were being deprived of their legal right to search for and obtain evidence, but the Escobedo ruling was nearly as unpopular. Professor Fred Inbau of Northwestern University Law School described it as the "hardest body blow the court has struck yet against enforcement of law in the nation."[8] The Escobedo case has generated a nationwide debate over confessions. Among supporters of the police and critics of the Supreme Court are former Attorney General Nicholas deB. Katzenbach, Professor Inbau, and New York District Attorney Frank Hogan; on the side of the Supreme Court, Judge David L. Bazelon of the United States Court of Appeals for the District of Columbia and Professor Kamisar. Professor Kamisar's defense of the Mapp decision applies equally well to the Escobedo case:

> What law-enforcement officers were really bristling about was tighter enforcement of long standing restrictions. Not Mapp, but state and federal constitutional provisions that had

[8] Chicago *Tribune*, August 11, 1964, p. 27.

been on the books for decades, banned arbitrary arrests and
unreasonable searches. The police never had the authority to
proceed without "probable cause," only the incentive. And
the principal contribution of Mapp was to reduce that incentive.[9]

In much the same spirit Donald C. Dowling, a National Defender Fellow at the University of Chicago Law School for
1964–1965, spoke for the Escobedo ruling

In deciding Escobedo, contrary to some popular belief,
the Supreme Court did not hold a wake for policemen; it
did not bury the confession; nor did it alter basic principles
of law enforcement. The decision did take up some of the
slack which some police have heretofore enjoyed in the
interrogation of criminal subjects.[10]

The Sixth Amendment states that "In all criminal prosecutions, the accused shall enjoy the right . . . to have the Assistance of Counsel for his defense." The logic of the Supreme Court is to confer this protection upon defendants in
state trials as well as federal trials, and to make it meaningful,
instead of a sham. To accomplish this the majority of the
court deemed it necessary to protect the accused at every
stage of the proceeding. In Gideon the right to counsel during the actual trial was affirmed. In Spano a strong concurring
opinion by Justice Douglas, joined by Justices Black and
Brennan and supported by Justice Stewart, held that the real
violation of constitutional rights was the refusal of the police
to allow the accused, after indictment and awaiting trial, to
confer with his lawyer. The Escobedo case in 1964 extended the right to counsel all the way back to the point

[9] Yale Kamisar, *op. cit.*, p. 323.
[10] Donald C. Dowling, "Escobedo and Beyond: The Need for a Fourteenth Amendment Code of Criminal Procedure," *Journal of Criminal Law,
Criminology and Police Science*, Vol. 56 (June 1965), p. 145.

when the police investigative effort shifts from investigatory to accusatory; in other words, a person in custody has the right to consult with counsel when he stops being merely a witness and becomes a suspect. On June 13, 1966 the Supreme Court carried the doctrine to its logical end in the case of *Miranda v. Arizona*, 384 U.S. 436 (1966). They held, in effect, that as soon as the police take a person into custody they must warn him of his right to remain silent and to have a lawyer, for whom the state will pay the fee if the person in custody cannot afford it. Oddly enough, the ground of this decision was not the Sixth Amendment, which guarantees the right to counsel, but the Fifth Amendment which protects against self-incrimination.

If Escobedo caused consternation among law-enforcement agencies, imagine their reaction to *Miranda v. Arizona*. It will cause no surprise to the reader to learn that proponents, both for and against the Supreme Court decisions, can cite "facts" to support their positions. For example, in analyzing one thousand consecutive indictments in Brooklyn from February through April 1965, New York Supreme Court Justice Nathan R. Sobel found that fewer than ten per cent involved official confessions made to the police. From this data, his twenty years of experience on the bench, and discussions with other judges, Judge Sobel drew the following conclusion:

> Confessions do not affect the crime rate by more than one one-hundredth of 1 per cent, and they do not affect the clearance (solving) of crime by more than one per cent.[11]

In another study of the court system in New York City, Abraham S. Blumberg reports that in the period from 1962 through 1964, of a random sample of 724 male defen-

[11] New York *Times*, November 20, 1965, p. 1.

dants who pleaded guilty to felony charges, fewer than six per cent had made confessions to the police.[12] The 724 defendants were asked who influenced them most in the final decision to plead guilty. Only four placed the responsibility upon the police, whereas 411 indicated that they were following the advice of their own defense counsel.[13] It is Blumberg's view (and one with which I agree) that the national debate over Escobedo reflects a false ideological perception of criminal proceedings. The focus of interest ought to be the bureaucratic structure of the court where more than ninety per cent of the convictions are negotiated by defense lawyers within an institutionalized setting of bargain justice.[14]

According to police officials and prosecutors, however, official confessions are not the only type necessary to police work. They maintain that seventy-five to eighty per cent of the convictions for major crimes rest on preliminary questioning that produces clues for further investigation.

If Mapp, Escobedo, and other decisions have had the effect about which police complain so bitterly,[15] statistics of arrests, prosecutions, and convictions, prepared and submitted by the police themselves, ought to reveal some impairment of efficiency. Table VII shows that in 1950, before any of these cases became law, police efficiency as measured by these traditional yardsticks was lower than it was after 1959 when Spano and other Supreme Court decisions began to restrict the police. Assuming the validity of these figures, one can conclude from the absence of gross variations in any year

[12] Abraham S. Blumberg, "Covert Contingencies in the Right to the Assistance of Counsel" (Paper read before the American Sociological Association, Miami Beach, Florida, August 30, 1966), p. 30.

[13] *Ibid.*, p. 33.

[14] *Ibid.*, pp. 3–9.

[15] For an incisive description of the fundamental police opposition to the Supreme Court decisions, see New York *Times*, September 5, 1965, p. 48; and Yale Kamisar, "When the Cops Were Not Handcuffed," New York *Times Magazine*, November 7, 1965, pp. 34, 35, 102, 105, 107, 109, 110.

after 1959, that the Supreme Court scarcely disturbed the even tenor of police work.

The Miranda doctrine will undoubtedly put more lawyers into the police stations to protect the rights of their clients from the very inception of police custody, and some confessions will be blocked, although it will be a very small number when compared to the total volume of cases. In a fair proportion of these cases the lawyer himself will see to it that his client pleads guilty in court. In all cases the police will be forced to improve their technique in order to gather proof of the charges without recourse to a confession. One great benefit will be to reduce the temptation to resort to illegal third degree tactics and thus to purge the police of a cardinal sin. Police practice under the Miranda rule will be routinized; the impact on arrest and conviction rates will be negligible. Any department worthy of being called professional will meet this challenge successfully and emerge the stronger for it. Within two months of the decision, evidence is accumulating to bear out this forecast, as "the police authorities of fourteen major cities conceded that it would not affect their procedures."[16]

To revert once more to our central theme, the real threat is not the shackling of law enforcement, but the probable

[16] Editorial in the New York *Times*, August 15, 1966, p. 26. Further corroboration for this point of view appeared in surveys conducted in Los Angeles and Detroit. As in the studies conducted by Judge Sobel and Blumberg, confessions to police were necessary for conviction in less than ten per cent of the cases, and "moreover, suspects are confessing despite advice by the police that they may remain silent and have free legal counsel if they are indigent." See New York *Times*, August 19, 1966, p. 20.

Ironically, despite their public protestations, in New York City detectives and commanding officers are secretly very pleased with the new state of affairs. Before these decisions higher authority always demanded better arrest and conviction rates, and no excuses could satisfy them. Now there is a perfect explanation for lower arrest and conviction rates—the necessity of observing all the safeguards and rights surrounding the suspect. This takes a great deal of pressure off them.

TABLE VII
A MEASURE OF POLICE PERFORMANCE

	1950	1959	1960	1961	1962	1963	1964	1965
Per cent of the known major offenses cleared by arrest *by Police in the United States*	15.3	27.1	26.1	26.7	25.7	25.1	24.5	24.6
Per cent of the known major offenses held for prosecution in court *by Police in the United States*	12.0	20.5	19.8	20.8	21.7	20.9	19.6	19.3
Per cent of defendants convicted in court as reported *by Police in the United States*	53.8	75.4	76.3	68.7	76.1	72.0	71.1	70.2
Per cent of the known felonies cleared by arrest *by the New York City Police Department*	*	35.2	34.5	35.3	35.5	34.9	33.9	34.5

SOURCE: *FBI Uniform Crime Reports*—1950, p. 14, Chart 8. 1959, pp. 81, 84. 1960, pp. 83, 86. 1961, pp. 83, 86. 1962, pp. 84, 87. 1963, pp. 93, 97. 1964, pp. 95, 101. 1965, pp. 97, 103. *New York City Police Department Annual Reports, 1959–1965.*

* The New York City Police Department's figure for the year 1950 is not entered because in that year there was a change in the method of reporting, and the police department's crime statistics were so unreliable that the FBI refused to accept them for inclusion in the *Uniform Crime Reports.* See Paul W. Tappan, *Crime, Justice and Correction* (New York: McGraw-Hill Book Co., Inc., 1960), p. 36, footnote 3.

reinforcement of cynicism among policemen. Each new reversal of hallowed legal principles upon which the code of police work rests, strips some of the majesty from the body of the law until at last the law becomes an emperor without clothes.

CHAPTER 7

Conclusions and Prospects

A series of vital questions remains to be answered in the future. Among competing ideologies of police administration, which will prevail? Is the police bureaucracy too rigid to adjust to the new procedures, attitudes, and values? What about corruption? What about civil rights? Can the police system survive intact under the pounding of the social forces of the metropolis? How will it cope with the condemnation by minority groups, the criticisms leveled by civil rights organizations, the clamor for civilian review of police action, and the United States Supreme Court's repudiation of the time-honored concept of law enforcement in the administration of justice? What are the prospects for the police establishment?

Professionalism remains an elusive goal, except perhaps, for a small minority of elite superior officers. As larger numbers of young men enter college and gravitate toward careers with more prestige than law enforcement, the preferred candidates who would be most receptive to the professional ideology diminish. Furthermore, until the occupational self-image and the public's view of the police become less divergent, proclamations of professionalism remain empty boasts.

True professionals—doctors, lawyers, and clergymen—preach that they are public servants, and the public pretends to accept this piety. Actually, both sides know that the professional is no servant, but is a leader, one of the elite of society. Yearning for professional status, the policeman likewise claims to be a public servant, although he too secretly pictures himself as a leader. Unfortunately for the policeman, however, the public takes him at his word: he is only a servant. Until the police can convince the public that they deserve a position of leadership, their aspirations to professionalism will not be satisfied.

According to the evidence submitted by investigation commissions over several decades, corruption is normal and probably inevitable in the police system.[1] Police administrators condemn all forms of corruption but are realistic enough in private conversations to admit that they cannot entirely eradicate it. Therefore, they are concerned with the questions of how much corruption ought to be permitted, and what types of corruption may be more acceptable than others.

During prohibition the police took graft from bootleggers and owners of speakeasies. Now, allegedly, the principal source of police graft is illegal gambling. If gambling is legalized and taxed to solve the desperate problem of municipal revenue, there will still be graft. Although generally tacit, a police consensus on graft does exist. For example, most policemen would not consider it wrong to accept a small Christmas gift from a friendly businessman on their post, or to eat a meal at a reduced price in a restaurant where they had done favors for the owner. Most policemen, on the other hand, would strongly condemn accepting money from a narcotics "pusher." I am convinced that the forms of graft

[1] Some authorities on the subject of municipal government believe that the Police Commissioner in time "accepts ultimately that police corruption is endemic to his organization, and that he is fortunate if he can prevent its reaching epidemic proportions." See Wallace S. Sayre and Herbert Kaufman, *Governing New York City* (New York: Russell Sage Foundation, 1960), p. 289.

quietly condoned by most policemen will prove impossible to eradicate.

Although they consciously fight corruption in the force, police professionals unwittingly create among some members of the rank and file a type of cynicism that excuses graft and resists the definition of police work as a profession or a vocation. If it is a business, the cynical policeman, like many Americans, may well feel that the important thing is "to make a buck." Alienated by the official ideology of the professionals, and resenting their condescension, the cynic retaliates by grasping any opportunity to make money as long as the force as a whole does not condemn it. Because these forces operate, no matter how high the salary, I believe (contrary to many authorities in police administration) that the best possible control of cynical corruption is the regular surveillance of police departments by independent investigating committees. Police administrators who consider themselves and their departments professional, should encourage periodic investigations, which prove they have nothing to hide.

Civil Rights

It is my firm conviction that the record of the police on civil rights, except in the South, is now far superior to what it has been.[2] The New York City Department, especially, has made tremendous progress. Despite this, the public image of the police force among minority groups has not improved

[2] For a statement confirming this opinion see Thomas R. Brooks, "New York's Finest," *Commentary*, Vol. 40 (August 1965), p. 35, in which he quotes an observation by Harold Rothwax, an experienced attorney in the Legal Aid Society, who said, "The actual use of physical force by the police is less frequent now than five years ago, and according to the old-timers around the office, even less so than twenty years ago."

to any great extent. If anything, it has deteriorated. Here is the self-appraisal disseminated by policemen (and ex-policemen) for policemen:

> Essentially, law enforcement in a democracy is one of the most humane services a human being can render to his fellows. It is a sign of the cynicism of our times that law enforcement is not universally accepted as a humane service either by police officers themselves or by the public.[3]

> The trend in recent years, however, especially in police training schools, has been to give wider recognition to the humane nature of police work. . . .[4]

Would anyone recognize the same enlightened law-enforcement agency in this bit of folklore by Langston Hughes?

> the musical term be-bop came from, so say jazz musicians—the sound of Harlem police clubs on Negro Heads.[5]

James Baldwin is more subtle, but more devastating. He concedes that the policemen are not evil. They are only blank, thoughtless, and doomed to be hated in Harlem, however positive their attitude. Despite some literary license, which causes him to overstate the gulf between the Negro community and the policeman, the following excerpt from Baldwin's writings is probably closer to the truth than the police would care to admit.

> Similarly the only way to police a ghetto is to be oppressive. None of Commissioner Kennedy's policemen, even with the best will in the world, have any way of understanding the lives led by the people they swagger about in two's and three's controlling. Their very presence is an insult, and it would be, even if they spent their entire day feeding gumdrops to children. They represent the force of the white

[3] A. C. Germann, Frank D. Day, and Robert R. J. Gallati, *Introduction to Law Enforcement* (Springfield: Charles C. Thomas, 1962), p. 186.
[4] *Ibid.*, p. 179.
[5] Langston Hughes, "Harlem III," New York *Post*, July 23, 1964, p. 29.

world; . . . Rare indeed, is the Harlem citizen, from the most circumspect church member to the most shiftless adolescent, who does not have a long tale to tell of police incompetence, injustice, or brutality. . . .

It is hard, on the other hand, to blame the policeman, blank, good-natured, thoughtless, and insuperably innocent, for being such a perfect representative of the people he serves. He, too, believes in good intentions and is astounded and offended when they are not taken for the deed. He has never, himself, done anything for which to be hated—which of us has?—and yet he is facing, daily and nightly, people who would gladly see him dead, and he knows it. There is no way for him not to know it: there are few things under Heaven more unnerving than the silent, accumulating contempt and hatred of a people.[6]

How successful have been the efforts of the police to ameliorate the situation? The New York City force is more humane; it observes the civil rights of Negroes more carefully than ever before. Its public relations program is concentrated on projecting a spirit of friendliness and decency, but that does not seem to have helped. In the past few years, New York's policemen have been subjected to unparalleled physical and verbal attack, especially from members of minority groups. Perhaps the answer is suggested by Murray L. Schwartz, professor of law at the University of California at Los Angeles, in his analysis of the Watts riots.

For the tragic fact is that for Watts the law is primarily an oppressive institution.

The most pervasive contact with the law in Watts is with

---

[6] James Baldwin, "Fifth Avenue, Uptown," in *Man Alone*, eds. Eric Josephson and Mary Josephson (New York: Dell Publishing Co. Inc., 1963), p. 352. For another expression of the Harlem Negroes' hatred of the police, couched in similar terms, see Kenneth B. Clark, *Dark Ghetto* (New York: Harper and Row, 1965), pp. 4–5. In New York City the Puerto Rican community is beginning to take the same view of the police; see New York *Times*, April 7, 1965, p. 45, and February 18, 1966, p. 18.

the police force, and one continuing, insistent complaint is of "police brutality."[7]

It is incontestable that for better relations with minority groups the police must constantly improve their record in civil rights. But such improvement, though necessary, may not be sufficient. Rapprochement must come from two sides and requires an ideological shift by the minority group. As long as the Negroes comprise an alienated ghetto society, the police will symbolize to them all that is detestable in an oppressive white social system. It becomes a vicious circle as the police respond in kind and

> the beating of arrested Negroes often serves as a vengeance for the fears and perils the policemen are subjected to while pursuing their duties in the Negro community.[8]

The police have relied on traditional methods that have not worked. What plan to break the cycle of hatred and violence is submitted by spokesmen for the Negroes? In the aftermath of the Gilligan case of 1964, James Farmer, then National Director of the Congress of Racial Equality (CORE), suggested a five-point program for the New York City Police Department "to prevent further tragedies of this nature and to restore confidence in the police force."

(1) Establishment of a civilian review board to investigate charges of police brutality.

(2) Screening of new policemen to weed out the emotionally disturbed.

---

[7] Murray L. Schwartz, "A Hard Lesson for the Law," *Saturday Review*, Vol. 48 (November 13, 1965), p. 36.

[8] This statement described Southern policemen but it describes the psychological response of Northern policemen as well. See Arnold Rose, *The Negro in America* (New York: Harper and Row, 1964), p. 177. According to Martin Luther King, the most serious charge against the police is that they permit organized crime—numbers, narcotics, and prostitution—to flourish in the ghetto. See Martin Luther King, "Beyond the Los Angeles Riots: Next Stop: The North," *Saturday Review*, Vol. 48 (November 13, 1965), p. 34.

(3) A review of regulations that require off-duty policemen to be armed.

(4) Better training in human relations for all policemen.

(5) Increased recruitment of personnel from minority
groups for the police force.[9]

These requests are so modest that the city could easily
grant them without restructuring the police department. But
would even the full implementation of the five points accomplish their purpose? Let us examine each proposal.

The concept of a board of civilians to investigate citizens'
complaints against the police was from the very beginning a
subject of bitter dispute. As established in New York in
July 1966, it had the limited power of inquiring into the
following types of civilian complaints: a) Unnecessary or
excessive use of force, b) Abuse of authority depriving individuals of rights guaranteed by law, c) Discourtesy, or
abusive, or insulting language, and d) Language, conduct, or
behavior which is derogatory toward a person's race, religion,
creed, or national origin. It was never intended to be a magical
solution to the problem of police-minority group relations.[10]
It had no power of prevention; its jurisdiction commenced
after, not before the act. It could only make recommendations to the Police Commissioner. Similar Civilian Review
Boards in other cities—Washington, D.C., Philadelphia, and
Rochester—have not had noteworthy success. Both sides,
the police and minority groups, have already condemned as
useless the Philadelphia experiment with a civilian advisory
board.[11]

[9] New York *Times*, September 3, 1964, p. 19. A short time before this
proposal, New York City Police Lieutenant Gilligan, while off duty, shot,
and killed a fifteen-year-old Negro boy who allegedly attacked him with
a knife.

[10] Sidney E. Zion, "Civilian Review Board Will Be No Panacea," New
York *Times*, May 8, 1966, Section IV, p. 5.

[11] New York *Times*, July 24, 1964, p. 9.

If the power structure in the police department truly believed that the department was as professional and above reproach as they claimed, should they not have welcomed public review to corroborate the fine record of achievement?[12] Many times commissioners have said that they want their force to guarantee the civil rights of minorities. For example, former New York City Police Commissioner Vincent L. Broderick, speaking for the benefit of the whole department at a promotion ceremony, warned his men:

> If you believe that a police officer is somehow superior to a citizen because the citizen is a Negro, or speaks Spanish— get out right now. You don't belong . . . in the Police Department.
>
> If you will tolerate in your men one attitude toward a white citizen who speaks English, and a different attitude toward another citizen who is a Negro or who speaks Spanish—get out right now.
>
> If you will tolerate physical abuse by your men of any citizen—get out right now.
>
> If you do not realize the incendiary potential in the racial slur, if you will tolerate from your men the racial slur—get out right now.[13]

This statement by Dan S. C. Liu, Chief of Police in Honolulu, Hawaii, provided the framework for a police executives' conference on "The Civil Rights Act of 1964—Implications for Law Enforcement" held August 7 and 8, 1964, at the University of Oklahoma:

> The primary objective of law enforcement is to give substance to those guarantees which promise every person his right to pursue his lawful business and pleasure in an orderly

[12] Although professional organizations proclaim their right to autonomy and self-policing, a civil service profession must concede the paramount right of the public to review its operation.

[13] New York *Times*, July 3, 1965, p. 16.

and tranquil society. The lawful exercise of the police power accomplishes this by respecting the dignity of the individual and embracing the concept of human equality under law.[14]

At that same conference the project supervisor of the International Association of Chiefs of Police, Nelson A. Watson, told the assembled police executives:

> We must refrain from all acts that are, in fact, brutal. I am sure everyone here will "buy" this statement: Any officer who would hit a man just because he is a Negro or who would use more force than necessary to effect an arrest just because the subject is colored is a disgrace to the uniform and should be dismissed.[15]

But police executives afterward resume their roles as leaders and defenders of the bureaucracy. Then they must contend with, and often come to share, the firm belief of the members of the force that many, if not most, accusations of police brutality and violation of civil rights are entirely baseless. A corollary to this, based upon the cynical lack of faith in the integrity of the civilian world, is the conviction that if a Civilian Review Board were to sit in judgment, it would automatically decide against the police officer. Thus Commissioner Broderick was impelled to battle Mayor Lindsay to "defend" his police department against the Civilian Review Board, although he was ordinarily a stalwart supporter of the rights of minority groups.

The facts surrounding the entire controversy are of interest, especially because they illustrate so well the material presented in this book. Mayor Lindsay during his campaign for election proposed a Civilian Review Board. In November 1965, as mayor-elect, he appointed a task force to study the

---

[14] International Association of Chiefs of Police, *The Police and the Civil Rights Act* (Washington, D.C.: International Association of Chiefs of Police, Inc., 1965), p. 1.
[15] *Ibid.*, p. 16.

police department and make recommendations for its improvement. One of the task force's recommendations was to create a Civilian Review Board composed of four civilians and three members of the police department.[16] Two days after the report of the task force was published, Commissioner Broderick wrote a seven-page letter to the mayor, and held a news conference, rejecting the proposal, calling it a cruel hoax, a bromide, an example of political expediency, and insinuating that it was an invitation to the mayor to take over the department.[17] (The reader will recall other examples of this bureaucratic fervor in Chapter 3.)

Mayor Lindsay, politically circumspect, waited until Commissioner Broderick's interim appointment expired, and then on February 21, 1966, inducted a new Commissioner, Howard R. Leary, formerly commissioner in Philadelphia. At last the head of the department was a man who accepted the principle of a Civilian Review Board, although it soon was public knowledge that he was not enthusiastic about it.

The chief objector to the Civilian Review Board was Patrolman John J. Cassese, the president of the Patrolmen's Benevolent Association. His official complaint stated that "the morale of the men on the force would be lowered, the power of the Police Commissioner diluted and the efficiency of all policemen impaired."[18] However, the true objection came to light with the appointment of the seven member board among whom were two Negroes and a Puerto Rican. Complaining of the four civilians on the board, Patrolman Cassese said:

> They're so pro-civil rights and so Lindsay thinking, I think Lindsay went out of his way to get these four.[19]

16 New York *Herald Tribune*, February 7, 1966, p. 1.
17 New York *Times*, February 9, 1966, p. 1.
18 New York *Times*, July 8, 1966, p. 19
19 New York *Times*, July 12, 1966, p. 33.

> [I am] sick and tired of giving in to minority groups.[20]

> Racial minorities would not be satisfied until you get all Negroes and Puerto Ricans on the board and every policeman who goes in front of it is found guilty.[21]

Is it the core of modern police psychology to equate those who are in favor of civil rights and those who are members of racial minorities with those who are automatically anti-police? Patrolman Cassese represents more than twenty thousand men, but we can only hope that in this campaign he was doing no more than speaking the language of the police minority—the subculture of cynicism. His polemics, the advertising he authorized, and the image he projected with its undercurrent of racism and rightism, proved that when the chips are down, the police rely on demagoguery not professionalism.

Members of the department who wanted to give the board a fair trial were branded traitors to the force. As soon as the Guardians Association, the Negro police fraternal organization, registered its approval of the Civilian Review Board, Patrolman Cassese at a news conference publicly accused them of disloyalty: "They put their color ahead of their duty as police officers."[22] If anything could lower morale and fan internecine conflict, it is this type of racist slur.

It was also claimed that the Commissioner's power would be diluted, although it is difficult to believe that the P.B.A. really cares about this power except insofar as they can reduce it further to their own advantage. The mayor had the authority to recommend the four civilians on the board, thus in some small way limiting the absolute freedom of the Commissioner to choose anyone he wanted. The second limita-

---

[20] New York *Times*, July 22, 1966, p. 15.
[21] New York *Times*, May 29, 1966, p. 42.
[22] New York *Times*, May 9, 1966, p. 29.

tion on the Commissioner's power was the fact that the board screened the cases before they came to the attention of the Commissioner and selected only certain ones for his consideration. Judge Francis T. Murphy of the New York Supreme Court disposed of both allegations in a decision announced June 23, 1966, in which he rejected the P.B.A.'s suit to bar the Civilian Review Board. The gist of his opinion was that the Commissioner may seek recommendations from anyone in whom he has confidence as long as the selection is not dictated to him. And furthermore, since the board's power is purely advisory, the Commissioner has in no way delegated or diminished his decision-making power.

Was the P.B.A. always so zealous a guardian of the Commissioner's authority? While all this was going on, the P.B.A. in its role of trade union was bargaining to take away the Commissioner's right to deploy men and materiel as he saw fit. Nor was the P.B.A. so protective toward earlier Commissioners. In a dispute with former Commissioner Kennedy, Patrolman Cassese took the position that the Commissioner was power-hungry, and needed to be controlled by a civilian board. In 1959 under the aegis of Patrolman Cassese the P.B.A. campaigned for a new law that would create a "committee headed by a civilian to review [the Commissioner's] decisions against policemen."[23] This bill, according to New York State Senator Basil A. Patterson, "would have done exactly what they're now fighting against."[24] The Commissioner's power was never the primary concern at all; it was a fight for P.B.A. power, police power, and perhaps the Conservative Party power. Commissioner Leary, no doubt touched by the P.B.A.'s concern for his position, took pains

[23] New York *Times,* August 9, 1966, p. 32.
[24] *Ibid.*

to reassure them that his power and authority was in no way impaired by the Civilian Review Board, nor was the efficiency of the department adversely affected.[25]

The accusation that police efficiency would suffer echoes an FBI report covering the riots during the summer of 1964, which stated in part:

> Where there is an outside civilian review board the restraint of the police was so great that effective action against the rioters appeared to be impossible. This restraint was well known in the community and the rioters were thereby emboldened to resist and completely defy the efforts of the police to restore order.
>
> In short, the police were so careful to avoid accusations of improper conduct that they were virtually paralyzed.[26]

These serious charges were directed against the cities of Philadelphia and Rochester. The minority groups denied that the police were restrained.[27] And Spencer Coxe, executive director of the Philadelphia branch of the American Civil Liberties Union, rebutted the criticism by calling attention to the reports prepared annually by the FBI itself, which indicate that during the seven years of the Review Board's existence, the Philadelphia police department has improved its efficiency to such an extent that it ranked near the top in this category. In Rochester the restraint of the police was widely praised because it exemplified the self-control of a truly professional force under great pressure and prevented permanent injury to the community.[28] There is merit to this policy, as shown by the decision of the New York City Police Department to institute a similar "hands off" policy

[25] New York *Times*, July 12, 1966, p. 33. See also New York *Times* October 17, 1966, p. 41.
[26] New York *Times*, September 28, 1964, p. 48.
[27] *Ibid.*
[28] *Ibid.*

"for thwarting massive street disorders"[29] during the summer of 1966.

If fear of being found guilty before trial does lower efficiency, as Patrolman Cassese would have us believe, then the P.B.A. is strangely silent in its appraisal of the Police Department's own Trial Room procedure. Here is the actual place of decision where cases, including those originally coming to the attention of the Review Board, would finally be tried. My own experience leads me to believe that at least eighty per cent of the patrolmen are firmly convinced that if they appear as defendants in the Trial Room, they will automatically be considered guilty regardless of the merits of the case.[30] Therefore, the disciplinary system within the department, rather than the Review Board, ought to receive attention as a focus of lower morale and efficiency.

Finally, the board had been operating quietly and efficiently for almost four months at the time of the November referendum. All reports proved that the board and the department were doing a fine job with every prospect of closing the gap between police and minority groups.[31]

On the basis of the material thus far presented, one could predict that if the Review Board had been continued (and it should have been), its net effect would not be great because the police bureaucracy would have routinized its procedures and absorbed its impact with Procrustean sophistication. But having failed, the board is more important than ever as a

[29] New York *Times*, July 25, 1966, p. 16.

[30] Item 9 of the cynicism questionnaire brought a response of C. from more than fifty per cent of the patrolmen and from forty per cent of the superior officers to the effect that they could not get a fair trial in the Trial Room.

[31] New York *Times*, October 18, 1966, p. 44. However, the vote against the board was really a backlash vote against minority groups. If this was the prevailing sentiment among the people of New York, what chance would the board have had to ameliorate conditions significantly?

symbol, not because it would have accomplished all that Mr. Farmer hoped, but because its defeat proves that when a police department grows so powerful that it can dominate an election, civilian review and control must be established as soon as possible.

The second proposal of the CORE program was to screen new policemen to eliminate the emotionally disturbed.[32] No one would quarrel with this. In New York City police candidates are already being checked for the presence of emotional disturbance: Investigation into the past medical and psychiatric history of the applicants is a condition of appointment. Medical examinations and stress interviews not infrequently lead to recommendations for psychological testing. Psychological tests of several different kinds are given to recruits at the Academy both as a routine practice, and also whenever there is any sign of serious disturbance.

It is of interest that just three weeks after Mr. Farmer's suggestion, Dr. Stephen McCoy, the chief surgeon of the department, announced that "a pilot project under which emotionally unstable policemen get psychiatric treatment has proved successful."[33]

There is an unstated assumption in this recommendation that Mr. Farmer would probably reject because it runs counter to the whole CORE philosophy. The implication is that at least one important reason for racial prejudice is emotional disturbance. Psychoanalysts would probably defend this statement, but as a political doctrine it would mean that CORE should be working for increased psychotherapy for bigots, either as a substitute for, or a supplement to, its present civil rights struggle. There is more than enough prej-

[32] One misleading implication of this proposal is that psychological or emotional disturbance is a rather important cause of police brutality and violation of civil rights.

[33] New York *Times*, September 29, 1964, p. 38.

udice in our society and culture to make it "normal" in the sense that most bigots may be typical Americans with no unusual emotional disturbance. A man of good will with an emotional disturbance is far less threatening to a Negro than a racist who is not at all "disturbed" as he wields the club.

Several large police departments are providing psychiatric examinations for all police candidates. Los Angeles has a model police force of five thousand members, with a fairly high percentage of college graduates, and every one of them has passed a thorough psychiatric examination. Would anyone allege that its record on civil rights is better than the record of the New York City police force? Does Watts have a higher regard for Los Angeles policemen than Harlem has for its New York counterparts?[34] It will take more than psychological screening and psychotherapy to cure a police force of prejudice and brutality.

The third remedy prescribed is a change in the regulations that now require off-duty policemen to be armed. From the standpoint of the minority groups who may fear possible police brutality, the off-duty member of the force is a minor threat, despite the Gilligan incident. For one occurrence of that kind there is an incomparably greater number in which policemen on official duty take part. This recommended change would hardly ripple the surface.

We come now to the question of better training in human relations. There is always room for improvement but for at least ten years the Academy curriculum has included a heavy

---

[34] In the summer of 1965 at a Police Civil Rights Conference in New York City, I had a conversation with a very intelligent superior officer of the Los Angeles Police Department, who was the epitome of professionalism. I asked him about the problem of police relations with minority groups in Los Angeles. He answered with perfect sincerity and absolute certainty that there was no friction at all. This conversation took place one week before the riots in Watts.

core of human relations courses. In addition, Unit training and refresher classes are given cyclically to the men in the precincts. The content of the offerings is of high caliber, incorporating the latest work of the social sciences. All instructors are accredited as lecturers in the City University of New York. Graduation from the Academy entitles the student policeman to ten credits toward a legitimate college degree from the John Jay College of Criminal Justice, of the City University of New York. Commissioner Leary, as if acting on this recommendation, has encouraged a new approach that will place civilian teachers and civilian experts at the Academy with heavy emphasis on human relations.[35]

One may say of this innovation, "It can't hurt." But the question remains, "Will it correct the problem?" Civilian instructors and experts are not necessarily better teachers than present Academy instructors. In talks on the complex subject of human relations there is always the possibility of a boomerang effect. What guarantees that a powerful course on the subject of human relations will change either police behavior or attitudes for the better? The plight of minority groups, at a time when education in human relations is sweeping the nation, is disquieting. Especially is this the case, if as Skolnick found in his study, it is true that "a negative attitude toward Negroes [is] a norm among the police."[36] The patrolman on post is constantly confronted with situations in which he has the choice of acting with consideration of human relations, or according to practical police techniques. In the majority of cases the average member of the force favors the resort to power. The role of the enforcer is still dominant.

Increased recruitment of minority group personnel would also be of some value. It would disprove the suspicion that

35 New York *Times*, June 22, 1966, p. 49.
36 Jerome H. Skolnick, *op. cit.*, pp. 80–88, 217–218.

there is occupational discrimination in hiring. But this still may not solve the problem of police relations with minority groups. For one thing it may be difficult to recruit large numbers of Negroes and Puerto Ricans. When a Negro policeman is called an "Uncle Tom" in Negro neighborhoods, not many young Negroes are likely to join the force. Once again Farmer's appeal was translated into action by Commissioner Leary. In March 1966 a police cadet program was developed with federal financial assistance under the Manpower Development Training Act. The plan was to train one thousand Negro and Puerto Rican youths for eventual appointment to the police force.[87] The project is in operation now, but fewer than two hundred students enrolled (as of Spring 1966).

If more Negro policemen were appointed, and assigned randomly throughout the approximately eighty precincts, their impact on minority group areas would hardly be noticeable. If, on the other hand, station houses in Negro communities were staffed principally with Negro policemen, it would seem a tacit acknowledgment that a predominantly white police force could not serve adequately. But Negroes are not immune from the pressures of police work. They are as vulnerable to *anomie* and cynicism as any other group on the force. If the white police officer swings his club in response to the thrust of organizational and occupational imperatives, will the nightstick of the Negro policeman fall more gently?

There is also the well-documented phenomenon of the man who demands from his own minority group a standard of behavior more stringent than that expected of others. He becomes so frustrated that he strikes out at his own people. Paradoxically, behavioral scientists claim to recognize in this

[87] New York *Times*, March 24, 1966, pp. 1, 35.

type of aggression toward others a classic illustration of "self-hatred."

CORE, as a representative of the Negro people, is completely justified in urging its own program for improving the police system, especially while Negroes remain the principal victims of injustice. But its suggestions are fairly orthodox; in fact, most of them are now in operation. The policeman's role of guardian and enforcer inevitably involves him in incidents that may be interpreted as police brutality. The solution to this problem is far more complex than some superficial modification of police personnel and procedure.

The degree of tension generated by such cases is an index of the power and alienation of the minority group. An apathetic response indicates high alienation and low power. As a result of the civil rights movement, a sense of militancy heightened by the slow pace of integration is easily converted to force under provocation.

In this context the police, as a symbol of white oppression, make an arrest at their peril.[38] Riot remains a threat. Rebuffed by white society, the Negro community accepts its alienation as a virtue, and in turn rejects the legal channels of protest.[39] Negro power is converted to force. Only when conditions vastly improve will Negroes be satisfied to test the sincerity of the white establishment by officially reporting cases of

[38] An analysis of all seventy-six reported race riots for the last fifty years up to 1965 concluded that the second most frequent precipitating incident was an arrest by, or an offense by, white law-enforcement officers against Negroes. See Stanley Lieberson and Arnold R. Silverman, "The Precipitants and Underlying Conditions of Race Riots," *American Sociological Review*, Vol. 30 (December 1965), p. 889.

[39] For example, with the defeat of the Civilian Review Board in the November 1966 election, the Negro community showed its lack of faith in police channels for review of civilian complaints. The N.A.A.C.P. set up its own civilian complaint review unit with four offices available to receive complaints against the police. See New York *Times*, November 10, 1966, p. 1.

alleged police brutality, and then waiting for the scales of justice to balance. Therefore, we may anticipate fewer incidents of police violence, at the same time expecting a greater number of them to come before a review board. That, in fact, was the experience of the short-lived New York City Civilian Review Board.

For several years the professional police elite has been consolidating the power that was so laboriously gained. Amazingly successful on promotion examinations because of their superiority in education (and probably intelligence), they reached a point where by sheer weight of numbers they saturated the highest levels of the department. The few remaining holdovers from the old regime made their peace and merged into the new order. Having mastered the bureaucracy's promotion system, the professionals were gradually accepted into the outgoing establishment they were destined to replace. But as they became a part of it, they were conquered by it. They found it expedient to continue many of the policies of the former power structure, to temper idealism with a more conservative policy that would not rock the boat.

With the advent of Commissioner Leary came the moment of truth for the new dynasty. Just as the professionals had challenged the fundamental values of the traditional police system, they, in turn, have been shaken by a series of rapid shocks. The first, and perhaps, most bitter blow was the appointment of an outsider from Philadelphia to head the department. The mayor thus disappointed many secretly hopeful aspirants among the top leadership, and they did not roll out the welcome mat for the new Commissioner. The second shattering of precedent was the appointment of Sanford D. Garelik, a member of the Jewish faith, to chief inspector, the highest position in the force, and one that had formerly been the monopoly of the Irish. The simultaneous selection of Lloyd G. Sealy, a Negro police officer, as assistant chief inspector, the highest rank ever attained by a Negro on the force, conveyed a clear message of new things to come. The strident, almost hysterical attack on these two excellent appointments, which the Commissioner had a perfect right to make, proved that under the veneer of professionalism the same old power struggles were raging, and that ethnic rivalries still inflamed members of the force.

Further confirmation was provided by the Commissioner's next innovation, the Civilian Review Board. The Review Board issue forced a showdown on the fundamental question: Can police professionals in good faith demand autonomy, or must they acknowledge their ultimate responsibility to the public they serve?

Before the Civilian Review Board crisis was settled, a new confrontation arrived in the form of a "hands off" policy to control street disorders. This was in direct conflict with strategy and tactics employed theretofore.

An exasperating reversal for the professionals to accept was the Cadet Program supported by the Manpower Development Training Act, because it concentrated on enrolling minority group dropouts. Professionals are still thinking in terms of police candidates with college degrees.

Another irritant was the Commissioner's eager agreement to further studies of the department by outside agencies. This policy violates the code of secrecy and casts a cloud over the reformation accomplished by professional leadership in the last few years.

The last disconcerting maneuver is the Commissioner's plan to introduce civilian instructors and experts into the Academy —that inner sanctum of police professionalism. Once they lose control over training and instruction of policemen, the professionals are deprived of one of their most powerful weapons in any long-range contest.

It is up to the members of the force to prove that the type of campaign waged against the Review Board did not represent the true face of police professionalism. The burden rests on the department to dispel the strong suspicion of minority groups that the police are their foremost enemy. It may be that the election results were in fact a Pyrrhic victory that will eventually bring stricter civilian review and control of police action, and there is a danger that certain dominant groups flushed by temporary success may become guilty of *hubris*, not realizing that the police system is now at the critical crossroad.

Fearful challenge and calculated risk are the parameters of police work in the protean, urban social order. The necessity of solving the problems delineated above, and of harmonizing the contending factions within the organization, will tax even the strongest administrative talents. Commissioner Leary's willingness to experiment and his refusal to be intimidated by the myths of law enforcement have already stimulated the entire police operation. Add to that leadership the support of the majority of the force who are men of intelligence and integrity, and there is reason to believe that the police department will move forward toward true professionalism.

APPENDIX

The Study of Police Cynicism

The Hypotheses

1. The degree of cynicism will increase in proportion to the length of service for the first few years, but it will tend to level off at some point between five and ten years of service.

2. Men newly appointed will show less cynicism than will recruits already in the Police Academy for some time. Recruits, in turn, will be less cynical than patrolmen with more experience. Not only will the average degree of cynicism be lower, but also the number of cynics in the group will be smaller.

3. Superior officers will be less cynical than patrolmen.

4. Among patrolmen, those with college educations will show a higher degree of cynicism than other patrolmen.

5. Patrolmen with preferred assignments (details) will be less cynical than other patrolmen.

6. Foot patrolmen will be more cynical than patrolmen assigned to other duties.

7. Patrolmen who receive awards for meritorious duty will be less cynical. Patrolmen who have had departmental charges lodged against them will be more cynical.

8. Jewish patrolmen will be more cynical than their non-Jewish co-workers.

9. When members of the force have seventeen or eighteen years of service, and they approach the time of retirement, they will exhibit less cynicism.

10. Members of the Vice Squad will be more cynical than members of the Youth Division.

11. Patrolmen with middle-class backgrounds will be less cynical than patrolmen from the working class.

The Questionnaire

The questionnaire consisted of twenty open-end statements concerning significant areas of police work. Three possible completions were listed for each item, and the respondent was instructed to select the option that, in his opinion, made the incomplete statement most nearly correct. In each case the first choice (a) was most closely attuned to the professional view of what a police department should be. The second alternative (b) was less extreme, representing a common-sense, middle-of-the-road approach. The last option (c) was a cynical or disparaging evaluation of the subject.

Numerical scores were assigned to differentiate among the selections. The choice of (a) was scored as 1; the second (b) counted 3; the last (c) was 5. If no selection was made for the item, a 3 was allotted. There were only 48 unselected items out of a total of 4,400 possible selections. The range of the scores for a completed questionnaire was from a minimum of 20 to a possible maximum of 100. Respondents who scored high were classified as cynics.

It is always difficult to prove the validity of a series of questionnaire items. It is submitted, however, that the items show a face and logical validity. As far as empirical validity is concerned, the results indicate that the questionnaire did succeed in dividing the sample into three distinct groups when they were measured by high, low, and middle range scores. In addition, the data support most of the hypotheses which had been formulated at least six months to a year before any possibility of a questionnaire presented itself.

Finally, I discussed the findings with experienced police officers. In their opinion, this study, if anything, has underestimated the true degree of cynicism that is rampant in the force.

THE CYNICISM QUESTIONNAIRE

In each of the following items, please circle the letter of the statement which, in your opinion, is most nearly correct:

1. The average police superior is _____
   a. Very interested in the welfare of his subordinates.
   b. Somewhat concerned about the welfare of his subordinates.
   c. Mostly concerned with his own problems.
2. The average departmental complaint is a result of _____
   a. The superior's dedication to proper standards of efficiency.
   b. Some personal friction between superior and subordinate.
   c. The pressure on superiors from higher authority to give out complaints.
3. The average arrest is made because _____
   a. The patrolman is dedicated to perform his duty properly.
   b. A complainant insisted on it.
   c. The officer could not avoid it without getting into trouble.
4. The best arrests are made _____
   a. As a result of hard work and intelligent dedication to duty.
   b. As a result of good information from an informer.
   c. Coming from the "coop."
5. A college degree as a requirement for appointment to the police department _____
   a. Would result in a much more efficient police department.

    b. Would cause friction and possibly do more harm than good.

    c. Would let into the department men who are probably ill-suited for police work.

6. When you get to know the department from the inside, you begin to feel that ———————

    a. It is a very efficient, smoothly operating organization.

    b. It is hardly any different from other civil service organizations.

    c. It is a wonder that it does one-half as well as it does.

7. Police Academy training of recruits ———————

    a. Does a very fine job of preparing the recruit for life in the precinct.

    b. Cannot overcome the contradictions between theory and practice.

    c. Might as well be cut in half. The recruit has to learn all over when he is assigned to a precinct.

8. Professionalization of police work ———————

    a. Is already here for many groups of policemen.

    b. May come in the future.

    c. Is a dream. It will not come in the foreseeable future.

9. When a patrolman appears at the police department Trial Room ———————

    a. He knows that he is getting a fair and impartial trial with legal safeguards.

    b. The outcome depends as much on the personal impression he leaves with the trial commissioner as it does on the merits of the case.

    c. He will probably be found guilty even when he has a good defense.

10. The average policeman is ———————

    a. Dedicated to high ideals of police service and would not hesitate to perform police duty even though he may have to work overtime.

    b. Trying to perform eight hours of duty without getting into trouble.

    c. Just as interested in promoting private contracts as he is in performing police work.

11. The Rules and Regulations of police work _____
    a. Are fair and sensible in regulating conduct off and on duty.
    b. Create a problem in that it is very difficult to perform an active tour of duty without violating some rules and regulations.
    c. Are so restrictive and contradictory that the average policeman just uses common sense on the job, and does not worry about rules and regulations.

12. The youth problem is best handled by police who are _____
    a. Trained in a social service approach.
    b. The average patrolmen on post.
    c. By mobile, strong-arm Youth Squads who are ready to take strong action.

13. The majority of special assignments in the police department _____
    a. Are a result of careful consideration of the man's background and qualifications, and depend on merit.
    b. Are being handled as capably as you could expect in a large civil service organization.
    c. Depend on whom you know, not on merit.

14. The average detective _____
    a. Has special qualifications and is superior to a patrolman in intelligence and dedication to duty.
    b. Is just about the same as the average patrolman.
    c. Is a little chesty and thinks he is a little better than a patrolman.

15. Police department summonses are issued by policemen _____
    a. As part of a sensible pattern of enforcement.
    b. On the basis of their own ideas of right and wrong driving.
    c. Because a patrolman knows he must meet his quota even if this is not official.

16. The public _____
    a. Shows a lot of respect for policemen.
    b. Considers policemen average civil service workers.
    c. Considers policemen very low as far as prestige goes.

17. The public ———————————
    a. Is eager to cooperate with policemen to help them perform their duty better.
    b. Usually has to be forced to cooperate with policemen.
    c. Is more apt to obstruct police work if it can, than co-operate.

18. Policemen ———————————
    a. Understand human behavior as well as psychologists and sociologists because they get so much experience in real life.
    b. Have no more talent in understanding human behavior than any average person.
    c. Have a peculiar view of human nature because of the misery and cruelty of life which they see every day.

19. The newspapers in general ———————————
    a. Try to help police departments by giving prominent coverage to items favorable to police.
    b. Just report the news impartially whether or not it concerns the police.
    c. Seem to enjoy giving an unfavorable slant to news concerning the police and prominently play up police misdeeds rather than virtues.

20. Testifying in court ———————————
    a. Policemen receive real cooperation and are treated fairly by court personnel.
    b. Police witnesses are treated no differently from civilian witnesses.
    c. Too often the policemen are treated as criminals when they take the witness stand.

The Sample

Even under optimum conditions there are problems in choosing a sample for a research study, then in persuading respondents to answer to the best of their ability. With policemen such research is twice as difficult.

The first great obstacle is that officers will not talk. There is no freedom of speech for members of the force. The surrender of this right is a condition of appointment, established as the law of the land by the legendary Justice Oliver Wendell Holmes, who at the time of the decision was on the Supreme Judicial Court of Massachusetts. The case involved a policeman who had been dismissed for discussing politics while on duty. He petitioned the court to order the Commissioner to restore him to duty, arguing that he had been penalized for exercising a civil right guaranteed to every citizen by the Constitution. The court denied the petition and Judge Holmes rendered the opinon that

> The petitioner may have a constitutional right to talk politics, but he has no constitutional right to be a policeman. There are few employments for hire in which the servant does not agree to suspend his constitutional right of free speech, as well as of idleness, by the implied terms of his contract. The servant cannot complain as he takes the employment on the terms offered him.[1]

The second barrier is the code of the job, which stresses secrecy and the confidential nature of police knowledge and opinions. Therefore, policemen frequently refuse to talk until they are ordered to do so by a court. Any questionnaire

[1] *McAuliffe v. New Bedford*, 155 Massachusetts 216, 220, 1892.

immediately arouses their suspicion and puts them on guard. They recall periodic investigations in which answers to questionnaires formed the basis of a prosecution against some hapless policeman. To overcome this reticence on their part is an art.

The sample consisted of 220 policemen. Thirty-four of them had been newly appointed and were, so to speak, a "naïve" group that was used as a control. The next major segment was composed of 60 probationary patrolmen, referred to as recruits. They had two or three months of experience and were still attending the police training school. The rest of the sample included 84 patrolmen, 15 detectives, and 27 superior officers from the ranks of sergeant and lieutenant.

It is my belief that the sample represented a fair cross section of an urban police department. The responses were, if anything, weighted in favor of professionalism.

Results of the Study

TABLE VIII
CYNICISM SCALE—RANK OF ITEMS BY TOTAL SAMPLE

1: highest cynicism; 20: least cynicism; N=220

Rank by Whole Sample	Topic of Item	All Police but Control	Control	Recruits	Ptl. 2–12 Years	Ptl. 13–19 Years	Detectives	Superiors	Original Item #
1.	Newspapers' attitude toward police	1	1	1	1	1	1	1	19
2.	Reason for departmental complaints	2	7	10½	2	2	2	2	2
3.	The attitude of police superiors	3	8½	9	5	3	8½	3½	1
4.	Is P.D. trial fair to policemen?	4	10	8	3	4	6	7	9
5.	Method of special assignments	5	12	3	6	5	3½	11½	13
6.	Qualities of average detective	6	13	4	4	7	11	6	14
7.	How policemen are treated in court	7	3	2	8	14	11	3½	20
8.	Policemen as judges of human nature	11	2	7	12	13	3½	5	18
9.	Why policemen issue summonses	8	18	15	7	6	5	9	15
10.	Appraisal of rules and regulations	9	14	5	11	10½	14	13	11
11.	An inside view of the department	10	16½	12½	10	8	7	9	6
12.	Public's attitude toward police	12	5	14	9	9	16	11½	16
13.	Best solution of youth problem	13	8½	10½	13	17	8½	14	12
14.	Effect of requiring college degree	14	6	16	14	10½	15	16	5
15.	Public's cooperation with police	16	4	12½	15	19	13	15	17
16.	Professionalization of police	17	11	18	17	12	11	9	8
17.	Police Academy training program	15	15	6	16	16	17	19	7
18.	Policeman's spirit of dedication	18	20	17	19	15	19	18	10
19.	How the best arrests are made	19	19	19	18	20	18	17	4
20.	The cause of the average arrest	20	16½	20	20	18	20	20	3

TABLE IX
CYNICISM SCALE

1 elicited highest degree of cynicism,
20 the least

Rank Order by All P.D. Groups Except Control

N=186. Average score for the 20 items=62.24

Rank	Subject Matter of Item	Score	Original Number in Question- naire
1.	The newspapers' attitude toward the police	3.87	19
2.	The reason for departmental complaints	3.77	2
3.	The attitude of police superiors	3.58	1
4.	Is a P.D. trial fair to policemen?	3.57	9
5.	How justly are men chosen for special assignment in P.D.?	3.54	13
6.	Qualities of the average detective	3.53	14
7.	How police are treated in court	3.43	20
8.	Why policemen issue summonses	3.25	15
9.	Appraisal of P.D. rules and regulations	3.19	11
10.	An insider's view of the P.D.	3.18	6
11.	Policemen's ability to judge human nature	3.16	18
12.	The public's attitude toward policemen	3.06	16
13.	How police ought to handle the youth problem	2.88	12
14.	Effect of requiring college degree for policemen candidates	2.83	5
15.	The outcome of Police Academy training	2.75	7
16.	Does the public cooperate with policemen?	2.735	17
17.	The professionalization of police work	2.731	8
18.	The dedication shown by the average policeman	2.42	10
19.	How the best arrests are effected	2.23	4
20.	Why a policeman makes an arrest	2.01	3

NOTE: Score above 3.00 indicates cynicism (items 1–12 above line).

TABLE X

CYNICISM SCALE

1: highest cynicism; 20: lowest cynicism

Rank Order by P.D. Control Group (First day at Academy)

N=34.   Average score for the 20 items=42.6

Rank	Subject Matter of Item	Score	Original Item #
1.	The newspapers' attitude toward the police	3.35	19
2.	Policemen's ability to judge human nature	3.18	18
3.	How policemen are treated in court	3.00	20
4.	Does the public cooperate with policemen?	2.88	17
5.	The public's attitude toward policemen	2.76	16
6.	Effect of requiring college degree for P.D. job	2.50	5
7.	The reason for departmental complaints	2.41	2
8.5	The attitude of police superiors	2.17	1
8.5	How police ought to handle the youth problem	2.17	12
10.	Is a P.D. trial fair to policemen?	2.06	9
11.	The professionalization of police work	1.94	8
12.	How justly are men chosen for special assignment in P.D.?	1.91	13
13.	Qualities of the average detective	1.909	14
14.	Appraisal of P.D. rules and regulations	1.59	11
15.	The outcome of Police Academy training	1.54	7
17.	Why a policeman makes an arrest	1.47	3
17.	An insider's view of the P.D.	1.47	6
17.	Why policemen issue summonses	1.47	15
19.	How the best arrests are effected	1.41	4
20.	The dedication shown by the average policeman	1.29	10

NOTE: Score above 3.00 indicates cynicism (only items 1 and 2).

TABLE XI
CYNICISM SCALE

1: highest cynicism; 20: lowest cynicism

Police Recruits, (2–3 months at Academy)

N=60.   Average score for all 20 items=60.27

Rank	Subject Matter of Item	Score	Original Item №
1.	The newspapers' attitude toward the police	4.10	19
2.	How policemen are treated in court	3.88	20
3.	How justly are men chosen for special assignment in P.D.?	3.58	13
4.	Qualities of the average detective	3.57	14
5.	Appraisal of P.D. rules and regulations	3.41	11
6.	The outcome of Police Academy training	3.31	7
7.	Policemen's ability to judge human nature	3.23	18
8.	Is a P.D. trial fair to policemen?	3.20	9
9.	The attitude of police superiors	3.13	1
10.5	The reason for departmental complaints	3.00	2
10.5	How police ought to handle the youth problem	3.00	12
12.5	Does the public cooperate with policemen?	2.97	17
12.5	An insider's view of the P.D.	2.97	6
14.	The public's attitude toward policemen	2.87	16
15.	Why policemen issue summonses	2.77	15
16.	Effect of requiring a college degree for P.D. job	2.69	5
17.	The dedication shown by the average policeman	2.51	10
18.	The professionalization of police work	2.50	8
19.	How the best arrests are effected	2.06	4
20.	Why a policeman makes an arrest	1.70	3

NOTE: Score above 3.00 indicates cynicism (items 1–9).

TABLE XII

CYNICISM SCALE

1: highest cynicism; 20: lowest cynicism
Patrolmen with 2–12 Years of Police Experience

N=42.   Average score for all 20 items=66.5

Rank	Subject Matter of Item	Score	Original Item #
1.	The newspapers' attitude toward the police	4.81	19
2.	The reason for departmental complaints	4.52	2
3.	Is a P.D. trial fair to policemen?	4.24	9
4.	Qualities of the average detective	3.98	14
5.	The attitude of police superiors	3.95	1
6.	How justly are men chosen for special assignment in P.D.?	3.74	13
7.	Why policemen issue summonses	3.69	15
8.	How policemen are treated in court	3.57	20
9.	The public's attitude toward policemen	3.43	16
10.	An insider's view of the P.D.	3.429	6
11.	Appraisal of P.D. rules and regulations	3.29	11
12.	Policemen's ability to judge human nature	3.19	18
13.	How police ought to handle the youth problem	3.05	12
14.	Effect of requiring a college degree for P.D. job	3.00	5
15.	Does the public cooperate with policemen?	2.76	17
16.	The outcome of Police Academy training	2.58	7
17.	The professionalization of police work	2.50	8
18.	How the best arrests are effected	2.33	4
19.	The dedication shown by the average policeman	2.21	10
20.	Why a policeman makes an arrest	2.19	3

NOTE: Score above 3.00 for items 1–13 indicates cynicism.

TABLE XIII

CYNICISM SCALE

1: highest cynicism; 20: lowest cynicism

Patrolmen with 13–19 Years of Police Experience

N=42.   Average score for all 20 items=62.7

Rank	Subject Matter of Item	Score	Original Item #
1.	The newspapers' attitude toward the police	4.48	19
2.	The reason for departmental complaints	4.14	2
3.	The attitude of police superiors	4.05	1
4.	Is a P.D. trial fair to policemen?	3.77	9
5.	How justly are men chosen for special assignment in P.D.?	3.55	13
6.	Why policemen issue summonses	3.43	15
7.	Qualities of the average detective	3.38	14
8.	An insider's view of the P.D.	3.24	6
9.	The public's attitude toward the police	3.14	16
10.5	Effect of requiring a college degree for P.D. job	3.09	5
10.5	Appraisal of P.D. rules and regulations	3.09	11
12.	The professionalization of police work	2.88	8
13.	Policemen's ability to judge human nature	2.80	18
14.	How policemen are treated in court	2.76	20
15.	The dedication shown by the average policeman	2.70	10
16.	The outcome of Police Academy training	2.60	7
17.	How police ought to handle the youth problem	2.51	12
18.	Why a policeman makes an arrest	2.41	3
19.	Does the public cooperate with policemen?	2.40	17
20.	How the best arrests are effected	2.33	4

NOTE: Score above 3.00 for items 1–11 indicates cynicism.

TABLE XIV

CYNICISM SCALE

1: highest cynicism; 20: lowest cynicism

Detectives

N=15.   Average score for all 20 items=58

Rank	Subject Matter of Item	Score	Original Item #
1.	The newspapers' attitude toward the police	4.47	19
2.	The reason for departmental complaints	3.93	2
3.5	How justly are men chosen for special assignment in P.D.?	3.53	13
3.5	Policemen's ability to judge human nature	3.53	18
5.	Why policemen issue summonses	3.43	15
6.	Is a P.D. trial fair to policemen?	3.29	9
7.	An insider's view of the P.D.	3.14	6
8.5	The attitude of police superiors	3.13	1
8.5	How police ought to handle the youth problem	3.13	12
11.	Qualities of the average detective	3.00	14
11.	How policemen are treated in court	3.00	20
11.	The professionalization of police work	3.00	8
13.	Does the public cooperate with policemen?	2.73	17
14.	Appraisal of P.D. rules and regulations	2.60	11
15.	Effect of requiring a college degree for P.D. job	2.47	5
16.	The public's attitude toward the police	2.33	16
17.	The outcome of Police Academy training	2.26	7
18.	How the best arrests are effected	1.93	4
19.	The dedication shown by the average policeman	1.70	10
20.	Why a policeman makes an arrest	1.53	3

NOTE: Score above 3.00 for items 1–9 indicates cynicism.

TABLE XV
CYNICISM SCALE

1: highest cynicism; 20: lowest cynicism

Police Superior Officers

N=27.   Average score for all 20 items=61.5

Rank	Subject Matter of Item	Score	Original Item #
1.	The newspapers' attitude toward the police	4.33	19
2.	The reason for departmental complaints	3.66	2
3.5	The attitude of police superiors	3.52	1
3.5	How policemen are treated in court	3.52	20
5.	Policemen's ability to judge human nature	3.48	18
6.	Qualities of the average detective	3.29	14
7.	Is a P.D. trial fair to policemen?	3.24	9
9.	Why policemen issue summonses	3.22	15
9.	An insider's view of the P.D.	3.22	6
9.	The professionalization of police work	3.22	8
11.5	The public's attitude toward the police	3.15	16
11.5	How justly are men chosen for special assignment in P.D.?	3.15	13
13.	Appraisal of P.D. rules and regulations	3.00	11
14.	How police ought to handle the youth problem	2.85	12
15.	Does the public cooperate with policemen?	2.69	17
16.	Effect of requiring a college degree for P.D. job	2.63	5
17.	How the best arrests are effected	2.55	4
18.	The dedication shown by the average policeman	2.48	10
19.	The outcome of Police Academy training	2.26	7
20.	Why a policeman makes an arrest	2.06	3

NOTE: Score above 3.00 for items 1–12 indicates cynicism.

TABLE XVI

SUMMARY OF RESPONSES BY SAMPLE GROUPS

Group	Number in Group	Total Number of Responses	% of choices that were		
			A	B	C
Total sample	220	4,400	31	39	30
All but control	186	3,720	26	41	33
Control	34	680	57	30	13
Recruits	60	1,200	31	37	32
Patrolmen 2–12 years	42	840	22	40	38
Patrolmen 13–19 years	42	840	23	45	32
Detectives	15	300	34	39	27
Superior Officers	27	540	26	45	29

TABLE XVII

SUMMARY OF RESPONSES TO ITEMS BY SAMPLE (EXCEPT CONTROL)

(N=186)

Questionnaire Item Number	% of choices that were		
	A	B	C
1	8	55	37
2	21	19	60
3	61	15	24
4	45	44	11
5	37	34	29
6	26	39	35
7	29	52	19
8	25	62	13
9	21	35	44
10	36	55	9
11	14	62	24
12	36	29	35
13	10	52	38
14	10	53	37
15	34	21	45
16	24	49	27
17	25	62	13
18	34	28	38
19	8	16	76
20	20	36	44

TABLE XVIII

SUMMARY OF RESULTS

Group	Number in Group	Standard Deviation of Group	Group Mean Cynicism Score	% of Cynics in Group	In Expected Direction	Level of Significance
Whole sample	220	12.9	59.2	43%	—	—
All but control	186	11.7	62.2	50%	—	—
Control	34	8.5	42.6*	3%*	yes	.01
Recruits	60	11.0	60.27	45%	yes	—
All patrolmen	84	11.6	64.6	56%	yes	—
Patrolmen 2–12 years	42	11.3	66.5*	64%	yes	.05
Patrolmen 13–19 years	42	11.8	62.7	46%	yes	—
Detectives	15	10.0	58.0	40%	yes	—
Superiors	27	13.4	61.5	48%	yes	—
Educated superiors: At least 2 yrs. college	15	13.1	58.8	40%	yes	—

Educated patrolmen:						
At least 2 yrs. college	23	9.5	69.3*	65%	yes	.10
Patrolmen with details	24	13.0	64.1	50%	no	—
Patrolmen in radio cars	17	9.5	61.6	47%	yes	—
Foot patrolmen	32	10.5	66.4*	62%	yes	.05
Patrolmen with 3 or more awards	17	9.6	58.5	41%	yes	—
Patrolmen 7–11 years	25	11.1	68.5*	72%	yes	.10
Patrolmen 17–19 years	11	13.7	58.0	36%	yes	—
Jewish patrolmen	10	11.7	71.9*	90%*	yes	.05
Patrolmen with 1 or more complaints	11	14.2	66.4	63%	yes	—
Unmarried patrolmen	7	7.6	73.4*	71%	yes	.01

NOTE: Base used for computation of significance was 62.2 for degree of cynicism, and 50% for number of cynics. This was mean score of whole group excluding the control group.
Cynic is defined here as an individual who scores above group mean of 62.2.
*Indicates that the difference between the starred score and the group mean is significant.

Analysis of the Results

1. The average police superior is ———————
   a. Very interested in the welfare of his subordinates.
   b. Somewhat concerned about the welfare of his subordinates.
   c. Mostly concerned with his own problems.

TABLE XIX

| Group | Number | % of choices that were | | |
		A	B	C
Total sample	220	13	54	33
All but control	186	8	55	37
Control	34	44	53	3
Recruits	60	13	67	20
Patrolmen 2–12 years	42	5	43	52
Patrolmen 13–19 years	42	0	48	52
Detectives	15	7	80	13
Superior officers	27	15	44	41

In this area of superior-subordinate interaction the professionally oriented training program has been indoctrinating superior officers with the personnel administration principle, namely that the good superior takes a lively interest in the welfare of his men. It seemed likely that professionals, or at least members who thought well of the department, would circle choice (a). It is notable that only eight per cent of the experienced members (which excludes the control group) picked (a). There are over three thousand superior officers in the department. Each patrolman may know fifty to seventy-five superiors well enough to estimate their degree of commitment. Knowledge of the other ninety-seven per cent depends upon rumor, known to be unreliable.

The control group also had no personal knowledge about superior officers to guide them in their decision. The responses of new appointees represent the opposite extreme. Only three per cent of them, one individual to be specific, chose (*c*). The superior officers themselves were divided in their reactions. It is of some interest that forty-one per cent of them took (*c*) as the most nearly correct completion.

ITEM 2

2. The average departmental complaint is a result of _____
   a. The superior's dedication to proper standards of efficiency.
   b. Some personal friction between superior and subordinate.
   c. The pressure on superiors from higher authority to give out complaints.

TABLE XX

| | | % of choices that were | | |
Group	Number	A	B	C
Total sample	220	27	19	54
All but control	186	21	19	60
Control	34	54	23	23
Recruits	60	37	26	37
Patrolmen 2–12 years	42	5	14	81
Patrolmen 13–19 years	42	20	5	75
Detectives	15	13	27	60
Superior officers	27	22	22	56

One indication of high morale is a respect for the organization's disciplinary system. The first choice (*a*) was consistent with such a view. Only the control group showed a majority who picked this over (*b*) and (*c*). Even (*b*) can be considered a somewhat derogatory opinion since, ideally, personal friction should be disregarded in the interests of impartial discipline. But (*c*) constitutes a completely cynical appraisal, insofar as the cause of the complaint is not related to accepted principles of administration, but to a desire to reduce pressure from above.

As with Item 1, patrolmen personally experience a very limited number of complaints among the many hundreds processed throughout a year. Since their opinions are only based on hearsay their choice probably reflects their own attitudes. Almost eighty per cent of the patrolmen group agreed with (*c*). The majority of superiors (56%) also selected (*c*).

ITEM 3

3. The average arrest is made because ――――――――
   a. The patrolman is dedicated to perform his duty properly.
   b. A complainant insisted upon it.
   c. The officer could not avoid it without getting into trouble.

TABLE XXI

Group	Number	% of choices that were		
		A	B	C
Total sample	220	64	15	21
All but control	186	61	15	24
Control	34	82	12	6
Recruits	60	79	8	13
Patrolmen 2–12 years	42	62	17	21
Patrolmen 13–19 years	42	52	24	24
Detectives	15	80	13	7
Superior officers	27	67	15	18

On the subject of arrests few respondents chose (*c*): a good arrest is highly prized. Moreover, a form of group solidarity exists that engenders reluctance to criticize a fellow worker in the performance of his principal duty.

ITEM 4

4. The best arrests are made ――――――――
   a. As a result of hard work and intelligent dedication to duty.
   b. As a result of good information from an informer.
   c. Coming from the "coop."

TABLE XXII

Group	Number	% of choices that were		
		A	B	C
Total sample	220	53	39	8
All but control	186	45	44	11
Control	34	85	9	6
Recruits	60	57	33	10
Patrolmen 2–12 years	42	40	52	8
Patrolmen 13–19 years	42	42	50	8
Detectives	15	53	47	0
Superior officers	27	38	44	18

This item explores not the motivation, but the method of making an arrest. There is a popular myth in police society that many arrests are made coming from the "coop" (a favorite location where a policeman sometimes goes to relax). The theory is that his chances increase for taking a criminal by surprise upon his return to post. However, the respondents did not confuse myth with reality. Few of them chose this option (*c*).

The second option (*b*) recognized the important part played by informants in building an impressive arrest record. When this is compared to (*a*) which accords due credit to the hard work and dedication of the arresting officer, it indicates a less romantic attitude toward policemen. Fifty-five per cent of the sample, excluding the control group, passed over (*a*) and in its stead, chose (*b*) or (*c*).

ITEM 5

5. A college degree as a requirement for appointment to the police department ―――――――
   a. Would result in a much more efficient police department.
   b. Would cause friction and possibly do more harm than good.
   c. Would let into the department men who are probably ill-suited for police work.

TABLE XXIII

Group	Number	% of choices that were		
		A	B	C
Total sample	220	38	35	27
All but control	186	37	34	29
Control	34	41	41	18
Recruits	60	38	38	24
Patrolmen 2–12 years	42	29	42	29
Patrolmen 13–19 years	42	34	29	37
Detectives	15	53	20	27
Superior officers	27	44	30	26

For the last ten years college men have been sought in every police recruitment program. Those who are working for professionalization consider them the hope of the future department.

The appointment of a man with a college degree should not cause friction unless it is the result of the attitude of those policemen who lack higher education.

One-third of the patrolmen thought that college men would be ill-suited for police work. An equal number felt that friction would result. Another third was of the opinion that the force would benefit from requiring college degrees. There is no doubt that each of the respondents taking a dim view of education for police candidates will give his own son the opportunity to attend college. It is not higher education *per se* that arouses resentment. This evaluation of education is specific to the police occupation and it is shared by two-thirds of the patrolmen.

ITEM 6

6. When you get to know the department from the inside, you begin to feel that _____
   a. It is a very efficient, smoothly operating organization.
   b. It is hardly any different from other civil service organizations.
   c. It is a wonder that it does one-half as well as it does.

TABLE XXIV

| Group | Number | % of choices that were | | |
		A	B	C
Total sample	220	34	36	30
All but control	186	26	39	35
Control	34	79	18	3
Recruits	60	31	39	30
Patrolmen 2–12 years	42	24	31	45
Patrolmen 13–19 years	42	21	45	34
Detectives	15	27	40	33
Superior officers	27	22	44	34

The police department of New York City is generally acknowledged to be one of the most efficient police organizations in the world. The control group, newly appointed, agrees substantially with this estimate. Seventy-nine per cent of them selected (*a*) which described the department as efficient and smoothly operating. A mere three per cent agreed with the last and very cynical observation (c).

Two or three months of experience in this department bring a dramatic change in attitude. Although they still know next to nothing about the way the system really operates, because they have been carefully quarantined in the Academy, the recruits have managed to assimilate a cynical orientation. In comparison with the seventy-nine per cent of the control group who thought that the department was efficient and smoothly operating, only thirty-one per cent of the recruit group was sufficiently impressed to select choice (a). Again comparing the same two groups, those brash enough to choose (c), which was a statement expressing surprise that the department does half as well as it does, increased tenfold from three to thirty per cent. For this shift, the theory of cynicism fits the facts better than any other. Over one-third of the sample (once again excluding the control group) adopted this position.

Ordinarily, one would expect superior officers to be more favorably disposed to the organization than men in the lower ranks. It is the responsibility of superiors to make the system function effectively. An unfavorable criticism of the operation is really a criticism of their own administration and supervision. This was not evident in the results because the superiors were split into very much the same percentages as the patrolmen. This can be interpreted as cynicism directed against themselves as well as against the department.

ITEM 7

7. Police Academy training of recruits ———————
   a. Does a very fine job of preparing the recruit for life in the precinct.
   b. Cannot overcome the contradictions between theory and practice.
   c. Might as well be cut in half. The recruit has to learn all over when he is assigned to a precinct.

TABLE XXV

Group	Number	% of choices that were A	B	C
Total sample	220	36	48	16
All but control	186	29	52	19
Control	34	73	24	3
Recruits	60	23	35	42
Patrolmen 2–12 years	42	26	66	8
Patrolmen 13–19 years	42	29	61	10
Detectives	15	47	47	6
Superior officers	27	41	56	3

The Police Academy enjoys a higher reputation than the rest of the department. It is ranked second only to the FBI National Academy. City University of New York grants ten credits toward a degree for students who have completed the four month course at the Academy. A joint committee composed of administrators and teachers from City College and the Police Academy supervises the curriculum and the methods of instruction, which are very professional.

The control group entered the department with the expectation that the Academy would live up to its reputation. Accordingly, three-quarters of them predictably circled the first statement to the effect that the Academy does a fine job of preparing the recruit. Only one of them (with no foundation for his opinion) agreed with (c) that the training might as well be cut in half.

After the two or three months' experience at the Academy, the recruits may be in a position to evaluate the Academy program. They may say whether they like it or not; in addition, they can tell whether or not it has helped them. But there is no way for them to know if their training will be useless in the precinct. Of course, it is not useless; without it they could not last a day in the precinct. Negative attitudes of this kind therefore are not based on fact. Their origin is in rumor and innuendo. The average recruit who selects the (c) answer is doing it because he is willing to doubt the value of a program presented to him as one of the best in the country. And significantly, he must be ready to doubt the integrity and veracity of the dedicated instructors who point out repeatedly that what they learn in the Academy may save their lives, or at least prevent their going to jail. The recruit group was most cynical of all; forty-two per cent of them picked (c) as the correct completion.

The middle, and usually neutral statement, in this item was loaded. When the Police Academy cannot overcome the contradiction between theory and fact, it is a serious fault. The individual who thinks this about the Academy program cannot value it very highly. Excluding the control group, seventy per cent of the sample accepted (b) or (c) as being nearer the truth than the only favorable appraisal (a). This leads to a conservative conclusion that a majority of the sample considers the Academy training a waste of time. Bruce Smith reported the same trend in his study of the department more than a decade ago. Then too, graduates repeatedly commented, "that attendance at the recruit school represents 'just a waste of time.'"[2] At that time the Academy had grave defects. As a result of the Bruce Smith report, the program was completely overhauled. It was the judgment of experts that the weaknesses were eliminated. Yet the negative view of the Academy is still dominant according to the data obtained by the questionnaire.

Possibly the disenchantment is justified by facts. Equally likely is the explanation that it is due to cynicism. This is more probable because the recruit group, which has the least evidence about precinct life to support its judgment, is strongest in its condemnation of the Academy. This lends weight to the inference that not objective conditions, but internal psychological processes are at work.

ITEM 8

8. Professionalization of police work _____
    a. Is already here for many groups of policemen.
    b. May come in the future.
    c. Is a dream. It will not come in the foreseeable future.

[2] Bruce Smith, *The New York Police Survey, op. cit.*

TABLE XXVI

Group	Number	% of choices that were A	B	C
Total sample	220	30	59	11
All but control	186	25	62	13
Control	34	55	42	3
Recruits	60	40	45	15
Patrolmen 2–12 years	42	29	66	5
Patrolmen 13–19 years	42	20	66	14
Detectives	15	13	74	13
Superior officers	27	7	75	18

In view of the tremendous propaganda campaign waged by the elite police groups for many years to convince members of the force that they are professionals, the results must be disappointing to the professionals. Less than a quarter of the patrolmen conceded that professionalism had arrived for many police groups. The reaction of the superior officers was unanticipated. Superiors are the main corps from which the professionals draw likely prospects. Just seven per cent of superior officers checked (*a*). More than twice as many (eighteen per cent), by choosing (*c*) revealed their cynicism by electing the statement that referred to professionalism as a dream that may never come. In general, however, the sample was neutral in that almost two-thirds expected professionalism in the future.

ITEM 9

9. When a patrolman appears at the police department Trial Room _____
   a. He knows that he is getting a fair and impartial trial with legal safeguards.
   b. The outcome depends as much on the personal impression he leaves with the trial commissioner as it does on the merits of the case.
   c. He will probably be found guilty even when he has a good defense.

TABLE XXVII

Group	Number	% of choices that were		
		A	B	C
Total sample	220	25	38	37
All but control	186	21	35	44
Control	34	47	53	0
Recruits	60	24	43	33
Patrolmen 2–12 years	42	0	42	58
Patrolmen 13–19 years	42	17	31	52
Detectives	15	60	13	27
Superior officers	27	33	26	41

The Trial Room procedure is closely modeled on the regular courtroom. The member of the force who is a defendant has the right to be represented by counsel. Rules of evidence are observed although not quite as rigorously as they are in an actual court. On important cases outside experts are asked to serve as trial judges. There is right of confrontation, right to cross examine, right to subpoena witnesses, right to make a statement not under oath, and right to appeal. Procedurally therefore, the trial is fair to the defendant.

The first choice (a) may be ambiguous because it refers to whether the patrolman knows that he is getting a fair trial, and not definitely to whether the trial itself is fair. The refusal to choose this alternative may mean either of two things: that the respondent feels that defendants have no faith in the trial procedure, or that the respondent himself considers the trial procedure unfair. This lack of faith is cynical because the trial procedure is from the legal standpoint as impartial as it could be made. The two possibilities are that either the members (eighty per cent) of the sample judge the police defendants to be cynical, or eighty per cent of the sample itself is cynical.

Not one of the forty-two patrolmen with two to twelve years of experience selected (a) as the correct answer. Less than ten per cent of the entire patrolman group felt that they were getting a fair trial. It is from this patrolman group that the bulk of the defendants come. The majority of patrolmen indicated by choice (c) that they expected to be found guilty even when they had a good defense. This is cynicism because it implies lack of faith in both the procedure and the men sitting in judgment upon them.

The superior officers rely on the Trial Room as the ultimate sanction with which to enforce discipline. They prefer the charges that eventually are heard in the Trial Room. They, at least, would be expected to show respect for this procedure. But only one-third of them chose the most favorable estimate (*a*). This is more than balanced by the forty-one per cent of the group who selected (*c*). In other words the superior officers who set the process in motion and are the complainants agree with the defendants that the trial procedure is unfair and prejudiced against the defendant.

ITEM 10

10. The average policeman is ─────────────
  a. Dedicated to high ideals of police service and would not hesitate to perform police duty even though he may have to work overtime.
  b. Trying to perform eight hours of duty without getting in trouble.
  c. Just as interested in promoting private contracts as he is in performing police work.

TABLE XXVIII

| Group | Number | % of choices that were | | |
		A	B	C
Total sample	220	44	49	7
All but control	186	36	55	9
Control	34	85	15	0
Recruits	60	28	67	5
Patrolmen 2–12 years	42	42	50	8
Patrolmen 13–19 years	42	29	57	14
Detectives	15	73	20	7
Superior officers	27	38	51	11

The same trend is apparent in the responses to this question. The control group exhibits the highest confidence in the organization and the members of the force. Eighty-five per cent of

THE STUDY OF POLICE CYNICISM

them take option (*a*) which praises the policeman for his dedication to the job. Not a single individual of this group chose (*c*) which was a completely cynical view of a policeman interested only in private contracts. The recruits with their usual cynicism, with no caution, but with ignorance, are the lowest of all groups agreeing with (*a*).

There was a general refusal to condemn the force by choosing (*c*). Less than ten per cent of the group did so. But if we examine the implications of statement (*b*), it is at once clear that only a cynic could say that what motivates the average policeman is a desire to stay out of trouble rather than a desire to do his job well, which is the gist of selection (*a*). A majority of the sample (except for the control group) indicated that (*b*) was the correct response. The desire to stay out of trouble may also be the principal motivation of the men who answered the questionnaires.

ITEM 11

11. The Rules and Regulations of police work ————————
    a. Are fair and sensible in regulating conduct off and on duty.
    b. Create a problem in that it is very difficult to perform an active tour of duty without violating some rules and regulations.
    c. Are so restrictive and contradictory that the average policeman just uses common sense on the job, and does not worry about rules and regulations.

TABLE XXIX

Group	Number	% of choices that were A	B	C
Total sample	220	24	55	21
All but control	186	14	62	24
Control	34	76	18	6
Recruits	60	15	48	37
Patrolmen 2–12 years	42	8	71	21
Patrolmen 13–19 years	42	8	77	15
Detectives	15	33	53	14
Superior officers	27	22	56	22

Less than ten per cent of the patrolmen believe that the rules are fair and sensible. Three-quarters of them are resigned to the necessity of violating rules in order to perform an active tour. The remaining individuals in this group say that the average patrolman does not worry about rules, and by inference, ignores them.

Superior officers undertake as their chief duty the enforcement of rules and regulations. Yet the great majority of them concur with the patrolmen in choices (*b*) and (*c*). How can a supervising officer legitimately enforce a set of rules which he admits that active policemen must violate? This is a dilemma for which no satisfactory solution is available. One mode of adaptation that reduces the level of tension is that of cynicism. The superior may disparage the men under him, or the system of which he is an important unit. From the responses of the superior officers in several of these questions, it appears that they are predisposed to do both.

ITEM 12

12. The youth problem is best handled by police who are ———
    a. Trained in a social service approach.
    b. The average patrolmen on post.
    c. By mobile strong-arm Youth Squads who are ready to take strong action.

TABLE XXX

Group	Number	% of choices that were A	B	C
Total sample	220	41	26	33
All but control	186	36	29	35
Control	34	67	6	27
Recruits	60	39	22	39
Patrolmen 2–12 years	42	39	21	40
Patrolmen 13–19 years	42	28	48	24
Detectives	15	33	27	40
Superior officers	27	37	33	30

The youth problem provides an opportunity to judge the orientations of the sample group because the topic, while of interest to policemen, does not arouse group loyalties or prejudices in the way that a more directly related occupational statement can do. The assumption was that the professionally oriented would choose (*a*) which recommended a social service approach. This is more like the policy of the Youth Division in the modern police department. The traditional view is that the patrolman on post is best equipped to handle the youth problem. The cynics deride the soft "do-gooder" social service philosophy. As they have no faith in the common man, choice (*b*) would not appeal to them either. The authoritarian reliance on strong-arm methods is attractive to them because when respect for men and principles is absent, force is substituted.

The control group fulfilled expectations by responding most readily to the professional solution (*a*). It is surprising that only six per cent revealed a willingness to rely on the policeman on post. The major sample was split into nearly three equal segments. Thirty-six per cent choosing (*a*) were sympathetic to professional standards. Twenty-nine per cent identified with the average patrolmen. And thirty-five per cent advocated the authoritarian approach of (*c*). This last group probably represents the hard core of cynics.

ITEM 13

13. The majority of special assignments in the police department ——————
   a. Are a result of careful consideration of the man's background and qualifications, and depend on merit.
   b. Are being handled as capably as you could expect in a large civil service organization.
   c. Depend on whom you know, not on merit.

TABLE XXXI

Group	Number	% of choices that were		
		A	B	C
Total sample	220	18	49	33
All but control	186	10	52	38
Control	34	65	29	6
Recruits	60	13	45	42
Patrolmen 2–12 years	42	8	48	44
Patrolmen 13–19 years	42	8	56	36
Detectives	15	7	60	33
Superior officers	27	15	63	22

Of all the administrative problems in the department, that of special assignments has been most extensively reformed. Assignments to detective and plainclothes duty, which are the prized details, are made from among men who have been recommended by their commanding officers for outstanding work. Then the candidates attend a long and difficult training course at the Academy during which they must pass several competitive examinations. Finally, their backgrounds are screened for signs of any lapse from good behavior. Only then will they be considered for such assignments. Every patrolman fills out a personnel data sheet with a list of special qualifications. This information is punched on I.B.M. cards. For important assignments electronic sorters find the best qualified men. Former Commissioner Kennedy was known to penalize any member who attempted to use the influence of a patron to obtain an assignment. However, all these reforms have been unable to eliminate the myth that appointments to desirable assignments are gained by resorting to a "rabbi" (an influential patron).

Consistently as ever, the control group perceived the department as a professional organization. Therefore, two-thirds of this group selected (a), which stated that merit was the criterion. But fewer than one-fifth of the remaining members of the sample concurred. More than one-third of the respondents decided that (c) was correct and that assignments depended on influence. This is an almost completely unjustified criticism of the method of determining assignments; the fault lies in the observer, not the department.

14. The average detective _____
    a. Has special qualifications and is superior to a patrolman in intelligence and dedication to duty.
    b. Is just about the same as the average patrolman.
    c. Is a little chesty and thinks he is a little better than a patrolman.

TABLE XXXII

Group	Number	% of choices that were A	B	C
Total sample	220	18	50	32
All but control	186	10	53	37
Control	34	59	35	6
Recruits	60	15	42	43
Patrolmen 2–12 years	42	2	44	54
Patrolmen 13–19 years	42	2	74	24
Detectives	15	20	60	20
Superior officers	27	15	55	30

The detective division enjoys the high prestige which is denied to the patrol force. Because of the new selection procedure, the detectives appointed in the last five years probably rank somewhat higher in intelligence and in dedication to duty than the average patrolman. With very few exceptions, patrolmen yearn to become detectives. Perhaps for this reason a certain envy of detectives is converted into a cynical derogation of their special qualifications.

This tendency was most strikingly evident in the fifty-four per cent of patrolmen with two to twelve years of experience who checked answer (c). This described the detective as "chesty" and convinced that he is a little better than a patrolman. It was surprising that only ten per cent of the sample other than the control group thought that detectives were superior to patrolmen. In contrast, the control group reflected a civilian public opinion, so that nearly sixty per cent circled choice (*a*). Only twenty per cent of the detective sample agreed that they were superior.

Approximately forty per cent of the recruits and patrolmen are skeptical about the merits of detectives and the system through which they are selected for this special assignment (see Item 13 above). These results assume greater significance when taken in conjunction with the very different official policy of the department. A New York *Times* reporter was told by a deputy commissioner of police that

> First-grade detectives are never selected by whimsy. Under the system of the Police Department, a man is promoted to any grade—whether it is first, second or third—because he knows the distinction that goes with it.
>
> A careful appraisal is made of any recommendation. That begins from the precinct level to the division level, to the borough command, to the chief inspector. And [Police Commissioner Vincent L.] Broderick makes the final decision.
>
> The Police Commissioner makes the selection for one reason: to propagate and keep intact the pride, common tradition and reputation of the Police Department. It's a tradition that the men take great pride in and have built up.[8]

This disparity of attitudes may reflect upon the character of complex organizations in which truth is generally relative to location and role.

ITEM 15

15. Police department summonses are issued by policemen _____
    a. As part of a sensible pattern of enforcement.
    b. On the basis of their own ideas of right and wrong driving.
    c. Because a patrolman knows he must meet his quota even if this is not official.

[8] New York *Times*, January 21, 1966, p. 18.

TABLE XXXIII

| Group | Number | % of choices that were | | |
		A	B	C
Total sample	220	41	20	39
All but control	186	34	21	45
Control	34	82	12	6
Recruits	60	46	19	35
Patrolmen 2–12 years	42	24	17	59
Patrolmen 13–19 years	42	26	26	48
Detectives	15	20	40	40
Superior officers	27	34	22	44

The existence of a summons quota for patrolmen is hotly denied by all police administrators, yet the legend persists that every patrolman is forced to issue a certain number of summonses each month to maintain his quota. Depending on the point of view, either one of the two contradictory assertions may be justified. No sensible commanding officer would ever tell the men in his command that they were expected to serve a definite number of summonses in any period. However, a patrolman with none or few to his credit would be questioned by his superior. In this sense there is an unofficial quota.

Police department policy is based on the need to reduce auto accidents and control traffic congestion. Summonses are a principal, if unpopular solution. Recruits are taught traffic law, service techniques, and the underlying philosophy of the enforcement policy. Refresher courses on summons procedure are periodically conducted for the others. The department is proud of its efforts in this direction.

In its replies to Item 15 the control group, as usual, was staunchly behind the department. They liked choice (a) which mentioned the sensible enforcement policy. Most of the recruits had never served a summons, having been instructed not to do so on practice tours except for flagrant traffic violation. Even so, more than one-third of them declared that a policeman issues summonses in order to meet his quota.

More than half of the patrolmen agreed with them that a

quota existed. Thirty-four per cent of the superiors selected (*a*) the sensible pattern, and forty-four per cent chose (*c*) the quota system. There is only one policy but evidently it is interpreted in different ways. The professionally oriented see it as sensible; the others discern in it the elements of a quota system.

ITEM 16

16. The public ———————
   a. Shows a lot of respect for policemen.
   b. Considers policemen average civil service workers.
   c. Considers policemen very low as far as prestige goes.

TABLE XXXIV

| | | % of choices that were | | |
Group	Number	A	B	C
Total sample	220	26	47	27
All but control	186	25	62	13
Control	34	35	41	24
Recruits	60	37	33	30
Patrolmen 2–12 years	42	12	52	36
Patrolmen 13–19 years	42	21	50	29
Detectives	15	33	67	0
Superior officers	27	15	63	22

In this question attitudes were mixed. The more cynical would deny a respectable public image of policemen. They would more likely choose the (*b*) or (*c*) alternatives. A realist may be expected to do the same. The occupational ranking consistently given to policemen in public opinion surveys is a little below the median. The group of approximately one-third of recruits and patrolmen who picked the most unfavorable choice (*c*) followed a response pattern so frequent that it is predictable: at least one-third of the respondents will always take the negative view of the department or of police work.

17. The public ————————————
   a. Is eager to cooperate with policemen to help them perform their duty better.
   b. Usually has to be forced to cooperate with policemen.
   c. Is more apt to obstruct police work if it can, than cooperate.

TABLE XXXV

Group	Number	% of choices that were		
		A	B	C
Total sample	220	27	58	15
All but control	186	25	62	13
Control	34	32	41	27
Recruits	60	22	58	20
Patrolmen 2–12 years	42	24	64	12
Patrolmen 13–19 years	42	36	56	8
Detectives	15	33	47	20
Superior officers	27	19	78	3

Seventy-three per cent (*b* plus *c*) of the sample did not trust the public to cooperate voluntarily with policemen. In their opinions the public must be forced to cooperate, and may even be obstructive. Oddly enough, this was the one statement in which the control group was more resentful than in any of the others.

What the respondents had in mind was not the public as such, but minority groups. As James Baldwin asserted (see Chapter 7) the police do sense the hatred of the people, and respond accordingly, rancor is symbiotic.

Personal tragedies as well as social catastrophes are the result. Enrique Negron, a Bronx grocer born in Puerto Rico, assisted a policeman at the risk of his own life when the former was attacked by an angry mob after trying to arrest a Negro youth. The police called him a hero, but Negron's own people turned against him. Because he had helped a white policeman, his neighbors boycotted Negron's store until he was forced to close.[4]

[4] A full account of this case can be found in the New York *Times*, January 17, 1966, pp. 1, 20.

18. Policemen ——————————
    a. Understand human behavior as well as psychologists and sociologists because they get so much experience in real life.
    b. Have no more talent in understanding human behavior than any average person.
    c. Have a peculiar view of human nature because of the misery and cruelty of life which they see every day.

TABLE XXXVI

Group	Number	% of choices that were		
		A	B	C
Total sample	220	32	29	39
All but control	186	34	28	38
Control	34	30	32	38
Recruits	60	37	22	41
Patrolmen 2–12 years	42	36	20	44
Patrolmen 13–19 years	42	29	40	31
Detectives	15	33	7	60
Superior officers	27	26	48	26

Choice (*c*) was intended to convey, through the use of "peculiar," the idea that policemen develop a cynical view of life because of their police experience. However, to those respondents who were more sensitive to connotations, "peculiar" may have meant "particular to the occupation" rather than "unusual" or "odd." Since there were so few college men in the group, it is unlikely that many of them chose the more sophisticated interpretation.

The average group response in favor of choice (*c*) was about forty per cent, a figure that is consistent with the pattern. Policemen apparently are aware that their occupational philosophy differs from the average one. That peculiar difference indicates cynicism.

19. The newspapers in general _____
  a. Try to help police departments by giving prominent coverage to items favorable to police.
  b. Just report the news impartially whether or not it concerns the police.
  c. Seem to enjoy giving an unfavorable slant to news concerning the police, and prominently play up police misdeeds rather than virtues.

TABLE XXXVII

| Group | Number | % of choices that were | | |
		A	B	C
Total sample	220	10	18	72
All but control	186	8	16	76
Control	34	21	41	38
Recruits	60	13	19	68
Patrolmen 2–12 years	42	5	0	95
Patrolmen 13–19 years	42	5	17	78
Detectives	15	7	13	80
Superior officers	27	11	51	38

Police departments are extremely sensitive to the power of the press, perceiving it as the barometer of public opinion. Because the police are involved whenever some emergency, crime, or unusual event of public significance occurs, their activities receive a major share of press attention. The best newspapers are impartial in their coverage of police news; tabloids sensationalize it. Some liberal newspapers often appear biased against the police when reporting stories about minority groups, civil rights, or juvenile delinquency. On the whole, however, newspapers treat the police fairly.

The results in this question confirm conclusively the defensive reaction of policemen to the press: ninety-five per cent of the younger group of patrolmen selected (c). Roughly three-quarters of the entire sample were in agreement.

ITEM 20

20. Testifying in court ─────────────
   a. Policemen receive real cooperation and are treated fairly
      by court personnel.
   b. Police witnesses are treated no differently from civilian
      witnesses.
   c. Too often the policemen are treated as criminals when
      they take the witness stand.

TABLE XXXVIII

| | | % of choices that were | | |
Group	Number	A	B	C
Total sample	220	20	38	42
All but control	186	20	36	44
Control	34	23	54	23
Recruits	60	13	30	57
Patrolmen 2–12 years	42	21	29	50
Patrolmen 13–19 years	42	29	40	31
Detectives	15	33.3	33.3	33.3
Superior officers	27	11	52	37

Policemen believe that the final test of efficiency comes with
the court outcome of a case. An arrest is validated only by sub-
sequent conviction. There is a certain amount of anxiety connected with the courtroom appearance of a policeman. If he
loses the case, there is the possibility of a damage suit on charges
of false arrest. As a witness the patrolman expects to be subjected to close questioning by the defense attorney. Some patrolmen imagine that a "payoff" or "fix" may cause them to lose
the case. Policemen think that the legal process is heavily
weighted against them and may feel hostility toward the court
system.

For this reason (c) was phrased to exceed a normal degree of
antipathy. To claim that a policeman is treated like a criminal is
a distortion of the truth that can only signify a completely
cynical interpretation of the facts. Of the sixty recruits, no more
than one or two had had any court experience as policemen.
Yet fifty-seven per cent chose (c) as the correct response.

About forty per cent of the other groups answered similarly.

It is obvious that the members of the sample, representing a cross section of the entire police force, are highly critical of the police organization. The group of one hundred and eighty-six men with some police experience preferred the highly derogatory (c) completion to the favorable (a) statement in twelve cases out of a possible twenty (Table XVII). In several other instances the (b) choice was popular although it was censorious. In the questionnaire as a unit, one-third of this group's responses were (c). Only twenty-six per cent (see Table XVI) of its choices were (a).

It is possible to be committed to an organization while criticizing its faults. Criticism becomes cynicism, however, at the point where it implies that responsibility for the conditions is due to stupidity, lack of integrity, and improper motivation. As an illustration of this phenomenon one need only set down the sense of the statements with which one-third or more of the experienced men agreed, although by doing so they discredited the organization.

1. The police superior is not very interested in the welfare of his subordinates, but is mostly concerned with his own problems.

2. Departmental complaints are given out by superiors not because they are dedicated to efficiency, but because there is pressure upon them to do so, which emanates from higher authority.

6. When you get to know the department from the inside, you begin to feel that it is a wonder it does half as well as it does.

9. At a police department trial the patrolman defendant will probably be found guilty, even though he has a good defense.

13. The majority of special assignments depend on whom you know rather than on merit.

14. The average detective is a little chesty and thinks he is a little better than a patrolman.

15. Police summonses are issued because patrolmen know they must meet their quota.

18. Policemen have a peculiar view of human nature.

19. The newspapers seem to enjoy slanting the news against policemen, and emphasize their misdeeds.

20. Policemen testifying in court are often treated like criminals.

In exactly one-half of the twenty statements comprising the questionnaire more than one-third of the sample (excluding the control group) chose the completion that was most critical of the police system, its personnel, or other agencies in contact with the police. For some of them it may be argued that even a person who is committed to the highest standards of police work may legitimately and severely acknowledge obvious short-comings. But commitment does not necessarily rule out cynicism. If the force believes that its criticisms are justified, they must inevitably conclude that the men responsible for these conditions are either very stupid or lack integrity. The majority of police-men accept this as part of the ineluctable system. Nevertheless, they fatalistically support the system they condemn, and cyni-cism is the catalyst that enables them to do so.

In this study only one of the thirty-four new men in the con-trol group was high in cynicism. The great majority of this group's responses were (a)—most favorable to the department. Newly appointed policemen evidently are ready to accept the idea that law enforcement is a profession.

This pattern altered in the case of the recruit group. Within two or three months the favorable attitude of the control group had disappeared, to be replaced by one of contempt and cynicism toward the organization. Forty-five per cent of this group scored high enough (Table XVIII) to be considered deeply cynical. The recruits had almost no personal experience of the matters under consideration. The knowledge they had was carefully censored and imparted to them by professionally oriented instructors at the Academy. It was part of a program to produce in the recruit group an attitude quite contrary to the one revealed by their responses. All that distinguished the recruits from the control group was their brief experience. This demonstrates dramatically how men change once they become policemen.

The Evidence for the Hypotheses

Hypothesis 1. Cynicism will increase with length of service, and reach its maximum at some point between five and ten years of service. Thereafter, it will tend to level off.

In order to test this hypothesis the population was grouped according to length of service, the only proviso being the inclusion of enough cases in each unit to overcome the effects of a few extremely deviant scores. The data of the superior officer and detective groups were omitted in this test because the respondents in these groups were concentrated in the thirteen to nineteen year group. In addition, the factor of promotion or special assignment to the detective division introduces an extraneous element beyond mere length of service. Therefore, the groups used were the controls, the recruits, and the patrolmen, yielding a total of one hundred and seventy-eight cases.

The graph (Figure 1) clearly delineates the steady growth of cynicism until the high point 69.1 is reached during the seven to ten year period. A more detailed analysis indicated that the maximum degree of cynicism among patrolmen was attained during the ninth and tenth years of service. During those two years the mean cynicism score was 71.3.

The control group on its first day at the Academy had a low score of 42.6. The recruits with only two or three months of restricted experience manifested a precipitous rise to 60.27. For patrolmen on the job from two to six years, there was a continued increase to 64.1. The average cynicism score for the seven to ten year interval moved to its highest point at 69.1. After this

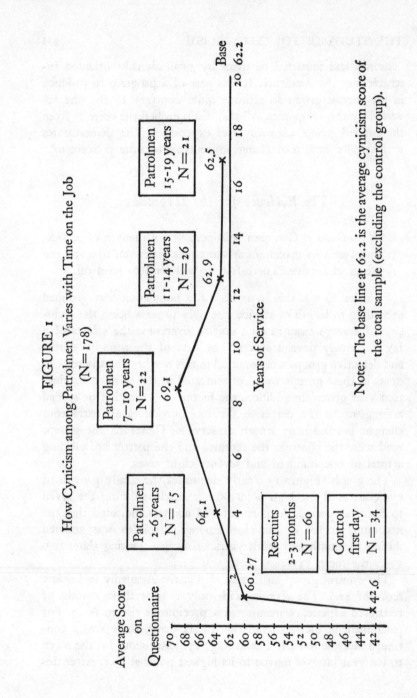

FIGURE 1

How Cynicism among Patrolmen Varies with Time on the Job

(N=178)

Average Score on Questionnaire

70
68
66
64
62
60
58
56
54
52
50
48
46
44
42

Years of Service

Base 62.2

Patrolmen 2-6 years N=15 · 64.1

Patrolmen 7-10 years N=22 · 69.1

Patrolmen 11-14 years N=26 · 62.9

Patrolmen 15-19 years N=21 · 62.5

Recruits 2-3 months N=60 · 60.27

Control first day N=34 · 42.6

Note: The base line at 62.2 is the average cynicism score of the total sample (excluding the control group).

a sharp drop occurred during the eleventh to fourteenth years, and the average score descended to 62.9. The trend then leveled off for the last stage of fifteen to nineteen years. The score decreased slightly to 62.5.

The true variable is not length of service. This is only an index of some correlation. More important is the nature of the impact of the occupation upon the policeman at each stage of his career, and this accounts for the change in orientation. Naturally, both length of service and age increase as he serves his twenty years, but his cynicism score fluctuates as a result of factors associated with the peculiar nature of police work.

When the sample means are compared to each other, the control group's score (42.6) turns out to be significantly lower than the mean score of any other sample group. This difference is significant at the .01 level (Table XVIII). Another important result was the recruit group's score (60.27), which was lower than the average score of the patrolman group (64.6), and this difference was significant at the .05 level.

Generally speaking, the first hypothesis seems well supported by the data.

> *Hypothesis 2.* Men newly appointed will show less cynicism than will new recruits already in the Police Academy for some time. Recruits, in turn, will be less cynical than patrolmen with more experience. Not only will the average degree of cynicism be lower, but also the number of cynics in the group will be smaller.

The control group—the new men—had an average cynicism score of 42.6. The recruits with only two or three months more police experience averaged 60.27. This difference was significant at the .01 level.

Comparing the recruits' score of 60.27 with the patrolmen's score of 64.6, it turns out to be in the predicted direction, and at the .05 level of significance. When the comparison is drawn between the recruits and the patrolmen with two to twelve years of experience who scored 66.5, the difference becomes significant at the .01 level. Of the more than ten special samples selected from the patrolman group for various comparisons, the average scores of all but two of these groups are higher than the score of the recruits.

The population mean for cynicism was 62.2—the average for the total sample, excluding the control group because they had no police experience. Those who scored above 62.2 were classified as cynics because they had higher than the average score. For the group of one hundred and eighty-six there was, therefore, a .5 proportion of cynics. The 62.2 and the .5 were used as base figures from which were derived the statistical tests of significance. The proportion of cynics in the control group— those who scored above the population mean of 62.2—was only three per cent. This was significantly lower than the proportion in any other group at the .01 level.

The proportion of cynics in the recruit group was forty-five per cent. For the patrolman group it was fifty-six per cent. This is in the predicted direction although not significant.

The evidence is consistent with the predictions of Hypothesis 2.

Hypothesis 3. Superiors will be less cynical than patrolmen.

The group of twenty-seven superior officers—nineteen sergeants and eight lieutenants—averaged 61.5 on the cynicism scale compared to a mean of 64.6 for all patrolmen. This is in the predicted direction although it is not statistically significant. In numbers of cynics the superiors again fulfilled expectations with forty-eight per cent of cynics as against fifty-six per cent for patrolmen.

This accords well with the hypothesis that promotion decreases the amount of frustration among superiors when compared to patrolmen who have failed the test for promotion. As a result, cynicism scores of superiors were predicted to be lower than patrolmen's.

The data are in the direction predicted by Hypothesis 3.

Hypothesis 4. Among patrolmen those with college educations will show a higher degree of cynicism because their expectations for promotion were higher than those of patrol-

men with less education. This leads to a greater degree of
frustration as long as they remain patrolmen.

Above all other groups of patrolmen in the department, college men are made to feel that they are failures because they
have risen no further than their uneducated colleagues. For this
reason it was predicted that college-educated patrolmen would
reveal more cynicism than average patrolmen. This would not
necessarily be true for college men who have become superior
officers, or even detectives, because these have received some
reward for their special qualifications.

Checking the scores of all patrolmen with two or more years
of college education, we find that the prediction of high cynicism is confirmed. The average cynicism score of this group of
twenty-three educated patrolmen is 69.3, significantly higher
than the total population mean of 62.2 at the .01 level.

Since this sample group was drawn from the group of eighty-
four patrolmen we may consider the patrolman group to be the
parent population for the purpose of applying the necessary
statistical tests. When the means of the two groups were compared, T equaled 2.3 which was significant at the .05 level. The
analysis was extended to compute the average score of the eleven
patrolmen with sixteen years of education. Nine of this group had
college degrees. As expected, their scores averaged 70.5, even
higher than the sample with fourteen years of education.

This is an important result because college makes an individual
more receptive to professionalism. It has been shown above how
the campaign for professionalization of the department is very
specifically directed to the college men. It might be reasonably
but wrongly assumed that the group most sympathetic to professionalism would be less cynical than those who are against professionalism. The frustration caused by failure to be promoted
is a more important determinant of a patrolman's attitude than
is his readiness to welcome professionalization. Therefore, in certain cases, education multiplies frustration and cynicism instead
of the reverse.

The scores of this college-educated group are also relevant
to the problem of whether authoritarianism of policemen is im-

planted prior to appointment by a process of self-selection, or whether it develops later as part of the socialization process. Supporters of the theory that authoritarianism is part of the personality before appointment should be consistent and acknowledge that high authoritarians are more susceptible than low ones to cynicism. It is well established, however, that the higher the degree of education, the lower is the degree of authoritarianism. It would follow, then, that the college-educated policemen, ostensibly low in authoritarianism, would be less cynical than the other patrolmen. We have seen that college patrolmen, on the contrary, are more cynical than other patrolmen. Where cynicism is concerned, frustration is a more important variable than either education or, by implication, authoritarianism. The conditions of life on the police force prevail over personality potentials.

The effect of education was masked by the frustration factor. What would happen if the frustration could be eliminated? To test this the detective and superior officer groups were chosen. Their degree of frustration on the job is lower than that of patrolmen because they have succeeded in the two great goals of every member of the force—promotion to higher rank, or assignment to the prestige-laden detective division. The same test of college education was applied to these two groups. Educated members scored consistently lower than the rest of the sample who had fewer than two years of college education. For example, the average score of the twenty-seven members of the full superior officer's group was 61.5. The educated superiors with at least two years of college—fifteen out of twenty-seven—had a mean cynicism score of 58.8. And similarly with the detective sample group, the educated detectives (only five out of the fifteen) had a very low score of 52, compared to the average (58) of the whole detective group. None of these was significant, although they were in the predicted direction.

Hypothesis 4 is well supported by the data.

Hypothesis 5. Patrolmen with preferred assignments will be less cynical than other patrolmen.

There were twenty-four patrolmen with special assignments other than the radio car. These jobs or details covered a wide variety of duties such as safety, clerical, plainclothes, youth work, etc. The results are rather inconclusive. The score of this group was 64.1, which was slighly lower than the 64.6 average of the total patrolman group. But it is higher than the mean of the older patrolman group—those with thirteen to nineteen years on the job. It is also higher than the total population mean of 62.2. Apparently, the majority of special assignments do not succeed in changing to any great degree the typical patrolman orientation. On the other hand, radio car patrolmen did affect a lower degree of cynicism. The seventeen members of this group scored 61.6, which was in the predicted direction but not statistically significant.

The evidence for Hypothesis 5 is inconclusive.

Hypothesis 6. Because foot patrol has low status on the job, foot patrolmen will be more cynical than other patrolmen.

The footman is at the bottom of the occupational pyramid. In several informal pilot studies made by the writer, members of the force were asked to rank various duties commonly performed by patrolmen. Foot patrol was always placed near the bottom. As a result the prediction followed that foot patrolmen, aware of their very low status, would feel more frustration than those assigned to more prestigious jobs. For these reasons it was anticipated that foot patrolmen would be high in degree of cynicism. This point is covered more fully in Chapter 3.

Their average cynicism score of 66.4 was higher than the population mean (62.2) and also higher than the average score of the total patrolman group which was 64.6. The score was not only in the expected direction; but also was significant at the .05 level.

Hypothesis 6 is supported by the data.

Hypothesis 7. Patrolmen who receive awards for meritorious duty will be less cynical. Patrolmen who have had departmental charges lodged against them will be more cynical.

If frustration leads to cynicism, reward and recognition may be expected to have the opposite effect. This was the rationale for Hypothesis 7. More than half the sample of patrolmen, forty-six in all, had received awards for meritorious duty. The ceremonies in which these awards are bestowed are special occasions of public recognition. The mayor of the city personally shakes hands with the recipients; the Commissioner donates a certificate; the press covers the function and publicizes it prominently. The award entitles a patrolman to wear a decorative bar on his uniform, and in some cases also carries money prizes. It allows for extra credit on promotion examinations, sometimes very substantial. A patrolman who receives one of these awards is made to feel somewhat above his peers.

With this in mind, expecting a low degree of cynicism, I tested the hypothesis, using as a sample all patrolmen who had received an award. No differences could be found between the scores of this group and the scores of other patrolmen groups. Then patrolmen who had received only one award were eliminated from the sample group and the test was conducted again for those who had received at least two awards. Still there was no discernible difference. Not until the group was restricted to an elite of seventeen patrolmen with three or more awards did an important change appear. Their score of 58.5 was considerably lower than the mean of the population, or the average of the patrolman group. The score was consistent with the original hypothesis, but it just missed being significant.

The detective group was anomalous in this respect. Awards are the rule, not the exception, in this division. It is a rare individual in this branch of service who does not have several awards. For example, fourteen of the total fifteen in the detective sample had been so honored. Seven of them had each earned six or more awards.

A test of the hypothesis was carried out on this group, and the results were just the opposite to what was predicted. Those with fewer awards also had lower cynicism scores. The seven who had six or more awards averaged 63, a full five points higher than the mean of 58 for the whole detective group. There are two plausible reasons for this reversal. The first is that the awards were the primary reason for the original low score of the detective group. Thus, the effect observable among patrolmen who had received several awards was hidden in the detectives' original response to the questionnaire, and could not affect the results a second time. The other reason is that awards are so common in the detective branch that they have lost their original significance. They may have become so commonplace that detectives hold them in contempt rather than in awe.

Although an award may be taken for granted, a complaint is a harrowing experience. The responses on Items 2 and 9 of the questionnaire proved how little faith the respondents placed in the formal disciplinary system.

This lack of confidence is so pervasive that it was one of the firmest trends upon which a hypothesis could be formulated. As a result it was predicted that patrolmen who had received a complaint would evince more cynicism than other groups of patrolmen. This was borne out by the data. The eleven patrolmen in this group ended with an average score of 66.4 that was well above the total population mean, and that of the patrolman group. This was in the expected direction although not significant.

Hypothesis 7 received some corroboration from the data.

Hypothesis 8. Jewish patrolmen will be more cynical than their non-Jewish colleagues.

The case of the Jewish patrolman has been examined in detail in Chapter 3. Their sensitivity to their own "Jewishness" and toward their low status inside and outside the department indicated deep-rooted frustration. Although there were only ten Jewish patrolmen in the sample, they more than fulfilled the prediction of high cynicism. Their mean score was 71.9, the second highest of any group selected for study. Nine of the ten were over the population mean and could be classified as cynics. This is a small number of cases and therefore does not command a high level of confidence, but these results were significant at the .05 level. The other groups did not have enough Jewish members to allow testing under varied conditions.

The results were consistent with the predictions of Hypothesis 8.

> *Hypothesis 9.* When members of the force have completed seventeen or eighteen years of service and they approach the time of retirement, they will exhibit less cynicism.

The foundation for this hypothesis has been developed more fully in the chapter on socialization. The veteran policeman has become accustomed to, and moreover expects a certain public deference. Upon nearing retirement he may discover when seeking employment elsewhere that his police experience counts for little in the competitive labor market. Police work thus assumes a new glamour and dignity; commitment is strengthened. Cynicism seems to decrease in respect to the police occupation, although it probably remains very strong in relation to the world and the public outside the police occupation.

The graph in Figure 1 illustrates the decline of cynicism in the later years of the police career. In Table XVIII it can be seen very clearly in the figures for the group of patrolmen with seventeen, eighteen, and nineteen years of service. The average cynicism score of the eleven patrolmen in this category is 58. That is lower than the score of any other group of patrolmen although the decrease is not statistically significant. In addition, the proportion of cynics was thirty-six per cent, which was smaller than that of any other sample group, except the control group. It was impossible to test this variable of experience with groups other than patrolmen because of insufficient samples in the seventeen to nineteen year category.

There is an alternative explanation for the above results: the reduced scores may result from a change in quality of cynicism rather than a reduction; advanced age is often accompanied by a sense of resignation.

Hypothesis 9 seems justified, although alternative explanations are possible.

Hypothesis 10. Members of the Vice Squad will be more cynical than members of the Youth Division.

The sample did not contain enough members of either division for the hypothesis to be effectively tested.

Hypothesis 11. Middle-class patrolmen will be less cynical than working-class patrolmen.

Class status is generally a significant variable in sociological analysis. The middle-class ethic favors the ideology of professionalism. The working class is less enthusiastic. Thus there was justification for the prediction that middle-class policemen would be less cynical. In order to ensure the unreserved cooperation of the respondents, the background information obtained was necessarily scanty. Extent of education was the only accepted criterion for allocation into classes, but since high school or equivalency diplomas were a condition of appointment, the variance here was limited. If two years of college education is established as a not very firm dividing line between working and middle class we may note some interesting observations.

Middle-class patrolmen, contrary to Hypothesis 11, are more cynical than working-class patrolmen. This is shown by the high score of the educated patrolmen (69.3). But middle-class detectives and superior officers are less cynical than their working-class peers. A policeman from a middle-class background, as measured by college education, is more receptive to professional ideals of police work. The evidence for this is the low score of detectives (52), and superior officers (58.8) who have at least two years of college education.

Middle-class membership, however, works well only as long as there is no intervening variable, such as frustration. Otherwise, middle-class status may change its valence, and the frustration may intensify the resultant cynicism.

There is too little data bearing on Hypothesis 11 to test its validity. Conflicting conclusions may be drawn.

Summary

Of the eleven hypotheses, eight are supported by the data, several of them with statistically significant results. Three of them (5, 10, 11) could not be properly evaluated owing to insufficient information. The variables postulated as significant in the etiology of police cynicism affected the results in the predicted direction. These variables were length of service, degree of frustration, and Jewish background. Corollaries were promotion, education, and number of awards.

There were two striking unanticipated results, extraneous to the hypotheses. The first surprise was that the seven unmarried patrolmen scored highest of all (73.4). Do policemen's wives affect their husbands' attitudes toward their occupation? Perhaps the degree of uxoriousness should be studied as a variable.

The other peculiar features was the factor of age. In intergroup comparisons age did not show any consistent pattern of effects. In intra-group analysis, however, the younger half of every group scored higher in cynicism than the older half. Length of service was not a question because the same trend obtained in the control and recruit groups. Whatever the effect of the age factor was, it was subordinate to and controlled by the other variables upon which the hypotheses were constructed.

Index